D1081082

'09

INTIMATE WITH THE ULTIMATE

INTIMATE WITH THE ULTIMATE

**Gerard and
Chrissie Kelly**

Authentic

MILTON KEYNES ● COLORADO SPRINGS ● HYDERABAD

Copyright © 2009 Gerard and Chrissie Kelly

15 14 13 12 11 10 09   7 6 5 4 3 2 1

First published 2009 by Authentic Media
9 Holdom Avenue, Bletchley, Milton Keynes, MK1 1QR, UK
1820 Jet Stream Drive, Colorado Springs, CO 80921, USA
OM Authentic Media, Medchal Road, Jeedimetla Village,
Secunderabad 500 055, A.P., India
www.authenticmedia.co.uk

Authentic Media is a division of IBS-STL U.K., a company limited by
guarantee, with its Registered Office at Kingstown Broadway, Carlisle,
Cumbria CA3 0HA. Registered in England & Wales No. 1216232. Registered
charity 270162

The right of Gerard and Chrissie Kelly to be identified as the Authors of this
work has been asserted by them in accordance with the
Copyright, Designs and Patents Act 1988

All rights reserved. No part of this publication may be reproduced, stored in
a retrieval system, or transmitted in any form or by any means, electronic,
mechanical, photocopying, recording or otherwise, without the prior
permission of the publisher or a licence permitting restricted copying. In the
UK such licences are issued by the Copyright Licensing Agency,
90 Tottenham Court Road, London W1P 9HE.

British Library Cataloguing in Publication Data
A catalogue record for this book is available from the British Library

ISBN-13: 978-1-85078-826-3

Unless otherwise stated, scriptures quoted are from The Holy Bible,
New International Version. Copyright © 1973, 1978, 1984
by International Bible Society. Used by permission of Hodder & Stoughton,
a member of Hodder Headline, Ltd. And the NLT.

Cover Design by fourninezero design.
Print Management by Adare
Printed and bound in the UK by J F Print Ltd, Sparkford, Somerset.

Contents

Introduction: The Jesus School of Prayer

In Eugene Peterson's *The Message*, there is a beautiful rendering of one of Jesus' most noted proclamations. In chapter 11 of Matthew's Gospel, we find Jesus deeply frustrated by the unbelief of the towns he has visited. But as he lifts his eyes to Heaven, he turns from frustration to prayer

> 'Thank you, Father, Lord of heaven and earth. You've concealed your ways from sophisticates and know-it-alls, but spelled them out clearly to ordinary people. Yes, Father, that's the way you like to work.'
>
> Jesus resumed talking to the people, but now tenderly. 'The Father has given me all these things to do and say. This is a unique Father-Son operation, coming out of *Father and Son intimacies and knowledge*. No one knows the Son the way the Father does, nor the Father the way the Son does. But I'm not keeping it to myself; I'm ready to go over it line by line with anyone willing to listen.'
>
> 'Are you tired? Worn out? Burned out on religion? *Come to me*. Get away with me and you'll recover your life. I'll show you how to take a real rest. Walk with me and work with me – watch how I do it. Learn the unforced rhythms of grace. I won't lay anything heavy or ill-fitting on you. Keep company with me and you'll *learn to live freely* and lightly.'[1]

Few passages in the gospel narratives offer such insight into the Jesus way of prayer. Long known and loved in its previous form as the invitation to 'take my yoke upon you', the passage has become even more meaningful to many readers since being morphed into Eugene Peterson's paraphrase. This eloquent rendering of the invitation to 'learn the unforced rhythms of grace' has become one of the truly memorable twentieth century contributions to understanding the spiritual journey. A new generation of spiritual seekers, moved by the poetry of these words, have been inspired to seek this grace whose rhythms are unforced and easy. For all the hard work of learning to pray there must be, they believe, a place of fluidity: a life in which the rhythms of knowing God flow freely and easily: where the obstacles to faith are overcome and the joys of living in God's presence are more evident than the trials of seeking him.

Imagine being asked to pick up and carry a backpack that is full to the point of bursting. It sits before you on the floor, promising a struggle ahead. But when you come to pick it up, a shock awaits you. Not only is it not as heavy as a bag of stones: it turns out to contain a helium-filled balloon. It is easier than you thought to lift and is itself a means of lifting. It is not the hindrance you expected, but a help. As you set out, aided by this unexpected joy, there is a spring in your step. The task you thought would be burdensome turns out to be a gift. Welcome to the Jesus school of prayer.

Invitation to apprenticeship

Peterson's elegant translation of this passage helpfully sets out the route in which prayer will take us. 'Walk with me and work with me,' Jesus says, 'watch how I do it' and you will learn what it is to take on a yoke that will not harm you. Jesus is not simply telling us where we are going, he is telling us how to get there. The education that is being offered here is apprenticeship – Jesus is inviting his followers into a contract of lifelong learning, an on-the-job training scheme in the ways of prayer. The Son of God, who is the Son of Man, invites us to learn at his side – to keep pace with him and find out what it is to connect with our Creator. This is not an invitation to some elite school of specialist spirituality; the divine equivalent of the SAS. This is Jesus the human, who has wrestled with manhood and Godhead and hearing his Father's voice, inviting his fellow humans to discover what he has learned. These are *life*-skills in the most fundamental sense possible – as basic as breathing; as vital as vitamins; as essential as exercise: daily skills in the development of a Godward heart. And the invitation is open to all. Unschooled, unskilled and unmotivated as you may be, this outward, open access world will accept you. The Jesus apprenticeship is an invitation into the most crucial covenant of all, the connection between creature and Creator.

Prayer is not an activity, it is a language. It is the language of a country we long for and have barely come to know, but in which we belong. The more we learn the language of prayer, the more native we become to the true land of our heart: it is in this outward, self-constructed world of darkness and self-management that we are alien. The first conversation ever to take place in human culture was a conversation between a man and his Creator. Prayer is the original heart language of humanity. When you speak the language of prayer you are speaking from the deepest part of yourself, from a created place so buried, so lost to us that its every word seems foreign. No wonder it's a battle. We have so forgotten who we are that the language of our birth seems strange to us. You were not created to be foreign to the things of God. You were made to be a native-speaker of prayer.

Walk

Jesus invites us to rediscover this language of the human heart in the three stages of learning brought out by Eugene Peterson's translation: *walk* with me; *work* with me; *watch* what I do. The learning contract offered begins with walking.

The foundation of our learning and the purpose of our praying can jointly be summed up in one word: relationship. 'This is a unique Father-Son operation', Jesus says, 'coming out of Father and Son intimacies and knowledge.' It is relationship with the Father that has given Jesus his unique perspective and it is into the intimate secrets of that relationship that he invites us. Discipleship and prayer alike are built on a foundation: relationship. Above all else prayer is conversation, the simple exchange of perspectives, needs and feelings. We may find it strange to think of God asking us 'Did you have a good day at the office, dear?', but such questions are not far from the kinds of intimacies Jesus is hinting at. This is about a sharing of our life. We are not in it for what we can get out of it and neither is our God. Speaking or silent; busy or at rest, this is a friendship in which to be in it is enough. The companionship of the journey is its destination and purpose. The foundation of prayer is relationship.

Work

Working cannot precede the walking, but must proceed from it. We do not work to gain relationship with our

God: that work has been done for us and is complete. But out of relationship there grows a willingness to work. There is intentionality to discipleship and prayer: a willingness to commit and make an effort. 'Come to me', Jesus says, 'Get away with me . . . walk with me and work with me.' This is focussed learning – Jesus asks for our attention. This is a call to active learning alongside the rabbi. It is a choice to follow; to imitate and emulate; to test and try.

Watch

Thirdly, Jesus hints at the fruit that will come from this foundational, intentional relationship. When we have learned to walk with Jesus, when we have worked at prayer at his side and grown in its practice, we are simply called to watch what God is doing. For the disciples who first heard these words, there is a direct and immediate application of this invitation. Jesus is with them. They can see with their own eyes what it is that he does each day. 'Do as you see me do' might be another paraphrase of this unique offer. But for those of us who are separated from the flesh and blood life of Jesus, there is another and deeper sense in which the call to watch might speak to us. Elsewhere Jesus has made the statement that his own life is guided by an unusual form of watching. 'I do only what I see the Father doing' he says.[2] Without living in the physical presence of the Father, Jesus is still able to see what he is doing. His life of intimacy and prayer renders visible the actions of the invisible God. And it is surely to this same privilege that we are called. And what is it that we will see when our eyes are tuned to the activity of God? Our gaze will be drawn to see the changes God is bringing to our lives and to our world. Prayer is founded on an unconditional relationship and fostered in an intentional path, but it is focussed on the outworking of God's purposes in the world. As we walk with God and work at his side, we are invited into the privilege of seeing him at work.

Prayerschool

Intimate with the Ultimate is an exploration of what it might look like to join the Jesus school of prayer today. What will it take for us to reconnect with this vital learning journey? In this age in which we know more, own more and yet are hungrier on the inside than any other generation, is it even possible to learn to pray? Can prayer become to us as easy as breathing?

We believe these things are not only possible but essential to human thriving. How else but by learning to pray will we learn to live? How else but by connection with our Creator will we escape from the crushing corruption that threatens to take our race and planet into darkness forever? To ask a human being to thrive without prayer is like asking a flower to bloom without the sun. It can't be done. We *need* this.

Our culture is passing through a period of intense and sustained change. Technological breakthroughs are transforming not only our industries but also our homes. In communication, successive waves of innovation have transformed the ways we connect. A philosophical tsunami has swept through education, changing what we teach and how we teach it. Globalization is redrawing the maps of our world and reconfiguring our worldviews. And a resurgent spirituality has brought new vitality – and new questions – to religions ancient and modern, opening up a century that many thought would be more secular than the last but has turned out to be less so.[3] In the storm of these changes, our churches struggle to find models of sustainable life and mission. New expressions and experiments abound. But whatever structures our churches settle into, whatever forms of faith we choose to pursue, one thing will not change. Prayer will remain the central avenue of our relationship with God. To know God is to pray and whatever else the faith-life of the twenty-first century will need, it will need a rediscovery of prayer.

24/7 *prayer*

There is evidence that a new generation understands this need perhaps more fully and more urgently than those who have gone before and *Intimate with the Ultimate* has been written in part from lessons we have learned by watching young people pray. Exemplified in the remarkable 24/7 prayer movement – a global awakening started 'by accident' when one young church in the UK decided to pray round-the-clock for a week – the early years of our century have been marked by a new wave of prayer amongst young people, a kind of global *prayershift*. Difficult to pin down to any particular denomination or stream, this wave has impacted young leaders in a wide range of ecclesial and missional settings, resulting in a renewed passion for God and his world. Young people are reconnecting with prayer as the central drama of their lives. In all its different expressions, this *prayershift* is built around the characteristics that the 24/7 movement so powerfully portrays: a commitment to extreme prayer for extended periods; a wild and creative approach that embraces art wholeheartedly and engages all the senses; a longing for justice and healing in the world; a willingness to pursue personal wholeness; a renewed commitment to God's mission locally and globally; and a determination to make prayer the very spine of life.

We have been thrilled to see this new awareness of prayer grow and have tasted the richness of its fruits. At a personal level, engaging in prayer in newly creative, heartfelt and committed ways has become a touchstone of God's presence. We still think and talk and read and network and reflect and plan and strategize: but we have discovered that it is in the surrendered moments of prayer, lying on the floor of a prayer room or gathering through the night, that clarity comes. This new movement is not a fad that will be with us for a while and then fade. It is, rather, an opportunity for all of us, perhaps especially in the churches of Europe, to re-engage with God's purposes for our continent and world. It is a heart-cry to the Father from a generation hungry for affirmation and significance. If our own experience is true – that through sustained, committed and creative prayer we can come to a clearer and deeper understanding of the will of God for our lives – then this movement may be the hope for all our futures.

True movements don't happen when a lot of people do what they are told. They happen when a lot of people do what they have not been told. Like a school of fish turning in an instant, a true movement relies on the combustion that takes place in each participant: each must bring their own energy to the party. This seems to be what is happening with young people and prayer. The potential for a fast-spreading movement is strong.

Intimate with the Ultimate has been shaped in part by our reflections on this remarkable movement and the elements that seem to be present in its many expressions. We have brought together seven threads we believe to be crucial for a rediscovery of dynamic prayer and available to each one of us to explore. These are arranged in terms of the three stages of apprenticeship set out in Matthew 11: the invitation to walk with Jesus, to work at his side and to watch what he does in our world.

In the first instance, we will *Walk* through the foundations of prayer. Here we will discover that the praying we are called to is **relational** and **rhythmic**

Relational because prayer allows us to *connect with our Creator.* No connection is more vital to our functioning as human beings and no relationship is more beneficial to our health. We were created for intimacy with God, born for this life of companionship and joy. And yet somewhere we have lost this simple key. In all the complexities of our techno-rich world, in all the multiple connections made possible by magic machines from the satellites that circle our planet to the phones that sing in our pockets, we have lost track of the simple capacity to walk with God. Can we recover the unadorned but life-changing reality of a relationship with our Maker?

Rhythmic because our prayers will be *earthed in the everyday,* a thread of spiritual life woven into the very fabric of our lives. The Jesus school of prayer does not ask us to add to our lives an extra layer of activity labelled 'spirituality' and disconnected from the rest of all we are and do. Rather, we are asked to establish the patterns and rhythms of prayer right in the middle of our everyday experience and to discover the spirituality that has always been possible. Not to escape the worldly for the heavenly, but to discover the holiness that the ordinary can bear when it is experienced in the company of Jesus. Prayer does not call us to a light that is 'over there' beyond the horizon of our dark world: it sheds light here. It is flesh and blood life we are called to.

Once we have discovered the *Walk* that is foundational to prayer, we will explore the *Work* by which the intentions of prayer are expressed. We will touch on prayer that is **restless, rich** and **reciprocal**:

Restless because we will find ourselves becoming *hungry for Heaven*, desperate to see a God-shaped world emerge within the skin of our experience. The further we walk with Jesus, the more we get to know him: and the more we get to know him the more fully we want what he wants. The great irony of Christian prayer is that it focuses us so fully on the earth and yet longs so heart-wrenchingly for Heaven: not in the sense of a place and time we would rather live, but in the sense of a reality that we long to see invade our here and now. The depth of the Jesus way of prayer can be summed up in the simple cry 'Heaven here: Heaven now.' It is a cry for the Kingdom to come, for the reign of God to flourish; for obedience to flow where rebellion has scarred the earth. Utterly motivated by the relationship that has grown from our walk with Christ, we find ourselves willing to embrace the work that our hunger calls us to.

Rich because we are *called to creativity*, invited by God to employ every colour at our disposal in this relationship of celebration and joy. The God to whom we pray – the Creator *with whom we converse* – is the Author of creativity itself. He is the source of colour and life, the one who went looking for a symbol to express his love for planet Earth and came up with a rainbow. Our God is the lover, the laugher, the juggler of joy and justice. He invites us to move beyond prayers that are addressed to him in the form of memos, in clipped language stripped of metaphor; colourless prose that expresses little more than our poverty of imagination. Can we learn to address and hear the starmaker in the infinitely creative language of his heart?

Reciprocal because in prayer we are *licensed to listen*, urged not so much to harangue God with our needs as to hear his heart for our lives. One of the most evident traits of the God Yahweh who comes to us as the God-man Jesus and continues in us by his Spirit is that he wants to be heard. God's commitment to self-revelation, his desire to communicate, is overwhelming. In the stories handed down to us that mark out the contours of his character, God is seen to shout and to sing; to whisper and to whistle in the wind. Time and time again he says to us 'Listen.' He speaks and every word takes us deeper into knowing our Creator and ourselves. To conceive of prayer as speaking to God, without ever acknowledging that he might speak in return, is to propose a spirituality that is sub-human and sub-Christian. The very thing that marks us out as human, the gift that most demonstrates the image of God in us, is that we communicate. The God who is and always has been the *logos*, the Word, has given us words to speak and hear. He is the essence of communication. Can we learn, in prayer, to hear as well as speak?

Lastly, we will explore the directions in which prayer moves as we *Watch* the activities of Jesus in our lives. We will come to see that prayer is **rooted** and **revolutionary**:

Rooted because we do not pray in a vacuum – we are *soaked in the story*, the inheritors of an adventure that has already begun. Just as God invites us to watch what he is doing in our lives, so to he allows us to see what he has done in the lives of those who have gone before. The stories gathered for us in our Holy Scriptures are essentially the record, over generations, of those who have done business with this God before us. From Adam and Eve, revelling in the presence of the Garden-maker with them, through Abraham and Jacob, Joseph and Daniel, Moses, Miriam, Deborah and Gideon; through David and Solomon; Isaiah and Joel; Elizabeth and Zechariah and Mary; through Luke and Paul and Peter to John, the apostle of love, alone on his island of old age, hearing the voices of Heaven as clearly as he might if he'd brought along his iPod and God was podcasting just for him: every one teaches something about what it is to walk and talk with God.

The later you arrive on the scene of history, the more you have the privilege of learning from those who have gone before. This faith, this great adventure of knowing and loving this Yahweh who is Jesus present to us by his Spirit, did not begin yesterday. It is a well-tried faith, both familiar and strange. The steps that lead to the throne room of God are worn down by the pilgrims who have climbed them already. To pray as if the story began with my birth is to commit a double error: firstly because it places me – my life, times, culture and understanding of the cosmos – at the centre of a drama to which they are at best peripheral, and secondly because it stops me from learning from those before me. I am a late entrant to a drama that has been running for eons already. Surely I will want to read the script, to know how things have been before I came on stage? And the script is Scripture. To pray without it is to misread the play entirely.

Revolutionary because the story that changes me will not end until it has changed my world. As God invites me to watch him at work, my eyes are drawn to three frontiers of his mission. There is an inward thrust of prayer that moves towards the *healing of my heart*. Prayer that is always linked to personal prosperity is not Christian in any meaningful sense of the word – no matter how often the name of Jesus is attached to it. It is pagan and belongs to the kind of praying the Bible seeks to un-teach us. But the great irony of our story is that the deeper we go into the self-denying fields of prayer to which God calls us, the more self-fulfilled we are. God denies us our foolish requests for wealth and fame because he loves us so much and has rewards for us that are so much better: like closing down a soup kitchen not because you want to starve the poor but because you want to take them all to the Savoy for dinner. Put in the simplest of terms, *prayer does us good* and the benefits of a life of prayer include the wondrous journey towards wholeness. Prayer promotes a revolution of healing in my heart.

By the same token there is an outward movement that calls us to the *rebuilding of ruined places*. Just as prayer leads me to wholeness; so prayer moves outward towards the healing of my world. I come to God hungry and thirsty. I am fed and I drink my fill: and I find my heart drawn to those who are hungry still. I bounce on the trampoline of forgiveness and remember those grounded by bitterness. There is an outward thrust to the true life of prayer that lifts my eyes, time and again, to the landscape of God's purposes: and that which is broken I long to see healed. Ultimately this calls me to *move into mission*, taking on God's passion for a planet-wide revolution. Prayer is not geographically defined nor spatially contingent. It invites me to travel to places my body may never visit. Prayer travel may well be the greatest extreme activity that our adventure-hungry culture hasn't yet found: the opportunity to go where the most committed back-packer and most wave-chasing surfer have never been. Wherever there are people, prayer has possibilities: its boundaries are as wide as the world; it will last as long as history itself; it is the ultimate never-ending adventure.

The Ultimate Connection

As we undertake this journey into prayer, weaving together these seven threads, we will come back time and again to our starting point: that this is a learning path for ordinary people. Prayer is not a specialized activity for certain followers of Jesus, only suited to some temperaments, a professional skill for pastors. Rather it is the essential language of human connection with God, basic to discipleship, with pathways in prayer suitable for each person. The plea of Jesus' first followers, 'Lord, teach us to pray' is the starting point for the journey of discipleship. Prayer is for every believer: as Richard Foster has taught, the heart's true home. To be human is to pray, living in radical dependence on the God who has formed and loves us and has plans that our small minds won't even grasp unless we let him open them. Learning to pray, then, is as simple as a child learning to walk.

Walk

In the end, we just had to give up and head home. Some of the others were hanging on in the city, hoping for some change, some news of the impossible but we couldn't stay with them. We both had work to do on Monday morning and besides, the corporate misery was getting somewhat heavy. It's all very well to come together to mourn the loss of a friend, but after even the greatest tragedy, life has to move on at some point.

It was mid-afternoon when we left the sad city behind us. Just getting out into the country air, the familiar road, the contours of rocks we had passed a hundred times, was some kind of comfort. He was lost to us, but the ground had not swallowed us; the world had not ended. And, mercy of mercies, we had at least been allowed to bury him. No such privilege had been afforded to the poor souls arrested as scapegoats of last year's rebellion: their bodies had been left in the sun to rot. By the time they were taken down there was little left to bury. How can you say goodbye to a brother or a son when you pass his disfigured and dehydrated body for weeks every time you come and go from the city? There was no 'rest in peace' for those poor families: three of them from our own village. Be thankful for small mercies – just the kind of thing my recently deceased friend would have said. Even in his desperation, he must have had some powerful friends for his body to be taken down so soon.

We walked more or less in silence. So much had been said already: what more was there to say? There hadn't been time to eat much today, we were hot and hungry: each focused on the relatively difficult task of getting one foot to move in front of the other and repeating the action a few thousand times to reach the threshold of home.

We stopped to rest awhile and take a drink at the olive grove near Seth's farm. There were others gathered there:

most, like us, on their way out from the city. The talk was all of the weekend's events. Some knew more than others. All knew something important had taken place. Crucifixions were not uncommon: but this one was ordered by Pilate himself, publicly. Alexander, an inn-keeper we knew well from our village, had been in the courtyard when Pilate pronounced sentence. 'I'm not sure what our leaders thought they were doing', he said to all who would listen in the grove. 'Didn't look like they had much of a will to save his neck. They're as bad as the Romans, that lot.' Quite a crowd had gathered for the flogging, many of them following all the way to the hill. Across the city the Romans were on some kind of alert, like the hairs of a fox standing on end. There was trouble in the air, though by today it had seemed that things were calming. A man I didn't know said he had heard that the troops in the villages around had been called into Jerusalem – he was convinced that the Romans were expecting another rebellion. Someone else I hadn't seen before asked if anyone knew why they had killed this man Jesus, but there were so many different answers piling on top of each other that nothing clear was said and most took the opportunity to get back to their journey.

We moved off from the grove in clusters, but these soon broke up as different ones settled into their pace. My brother and I found ourselves walking with just one other traveller, the one who had asked about the reason for Jesus' death. He was definitely not from our village, though it seemed he had business there. He said nothing for a while, settling into his own step alongside us. But then he asked us the strangest of questions.

'What were they all talking about, back there at the grove?'

'Who do you mean?' I asked.

'Everyone', he said, 'Talking about this crucifixion; the fear of rebellion . . . there seems to have been quite some events these past days.'

I couldn't believe he didn't know what had been happening. Where had he been the whole weekend? You'd have to have been drunk or drugged to have missed the talk in the City since Friday.

'You must be the only one who doesn't know', my brother said, perhaps a little too abruptly. My brother was not known for the subtlety of his conversation.

'Tell me', he said. And so we did – the whole story. Once we started, we couldn't stop. It all came out: the hopes we had had of our Messiah; the strange things we had allowed ourselves to believe; the way it had all ended in such bloody dismay on Friday. Oddly, it was therapeutic to talk to someone who knew nothing of the story and he seemed to know this. He let us talk, on and on, encouraging us with the occasional nod, asking questions when something we were saying wasn't clear. By the time our story got to Sunday morning, I had begun to feel lighter in my spirit than I had for days.

The last part of the story was little more than an afterthought. Some of the women had gone to the tomb at sunrise to anoint the body and came running to say that it was gone. Peter and one or two others went to see and they, too, said that the body was gone but we didn't know what to make of it. By that time there had been so many rumours and counter-rumours, I just couldn't take any more on board. I half wondered if they had gone to the wrong tomb: it had all been arranged in such a rush on Friday, with the Sabbath just moments away. In the confusion of the past few days, I wouldn't put it past any of us to make such a mistake.

Our friend didn't seem too taken with this explanation but he was deep in thought. Then he turned to me and asked the second strange question of the day.

'Can't you see?' he asked, 'It all makes perfect sense.' And before I could answer, he explained that Jesus could indeed have been the Messiah we were waiting for, because our Scriptures had always told us that the Messiah would suffer and die.

This was news to me, but he backed it up with lines from Moses and Job and the psalms; even the psalm Jesus was said to have recited with his dying breath. It was incredible. For a moment it was like having Jesus back with us – I had never heard the Scriptures talked about this way by anyone else. The stories came alive – not like the dry pronouncements we hear week by week in the synagogue. By the time we were within sight of home, he had me believing that Jesus might indeed still be our Messiah. Something I had never dreamed possible – that the Chosen one of God would suffer death – turned out to be the very thing our Scriptures had been saying for centuries. When he quoted from Isaiah – the song of the sufferings of Israel – I could hardly believe my ears. I had known these words from my earliest years. I had never seen that they could mean what I now saw for certain that they must mean. Why had these words not come to my mind when I had watched Jesus die? Now, on the road home, hearing them recited by this stranger, was like reliving Friday. I could see Jesus in my mind – those terrible images that will never leave me as long as I live – and the words fitted. It was as if they were partners separated for years – the words and images – but now brought together again and as soon as they were reunited, it was undeniable that they belonged together. But if that was so, if God had spoken centuries ago in a way that so directly and perfectly described Jesus, then perhaps it was not all so unintended . . . perhaps God had meant all along . . .

It was almost too much to think about. The miles from the orange grove to home had been eaten up in the intensity of our conversation. Surely the strangest walk I have ever taken. But the light was failing as we drew near to the village and it didn't seem that our remarkable friend had anywhere to stay. My brother insisted he come to us. I would have said the same but my brother is usually first in such offers – and he is not easy to refuse. Before our companion

*had even begun to say that he wouldn't want to trouble us,
it had been made clear that it was no trouble and that 'No'
was not an acceptable response.*

*'I insist', my brother said emphatically.'It has been a long
day and a long walk, none of us has eaten and I have many
more questions to ask you. There is shelter and a room to spare
with us – you will be an honoured guest in our home. Come
and break bread with us . . .'*

Why walk?

The story of the road to Emmaus, recorded in chapter 24
of the Gospel of Luke, takes pride of place there as one
of the most compelling of the resurrection narratives.
The two disciples would later gasp that their hearts
'burned within them' as the unrecognized Jesus spoke
with them. Having already pressed him to stay with
them because the night was falling and it was too dangerous to travel, they head back to Jerusalem – nightfall
or no nightfall – to share with Peter and the others the
remarkable news they have discovered. Jesus is the
Messiah and Jesus is alive.

Two disciples, unnamed and unmentioned anywhere
else in Scripture, who play no part in the pre-crucifixion
gospel narratives and have no role among the twelve,
take centre stage in what is perhaps the most important
section of Luke's narrative: the assertion that Jesus is
risen. Does Luke tell the tale this way for a reason? Is it
important that we realize, from the very moment of the
resurrection, that this is news for all the world? The

resurrection of Jesus is not significant only for those who have been close to him in his earthly ministry. It is not just for the impetuous Peter, the romantic John, the questioning Thomas: it is for all those who will believe. For the early readers of Luke's Gospel, it is quite possible that Cleopas and his companion play this important role because they represent the first of those outside the inner circle of Jesus' followers who receive the news of the resurrection. They were doubtless known figures in the Early Church and so would be seen as 'the first of us': the beginnings of the revolution that would take the news of Jesus' death and resurrection from being something his friends and loved ones might like to know to being something we all need to hear. They are the 'Everyman' of Luke's story: who on behalf of all of us steps onto the stage and into the action to interpret the play for ordinary people. And as such, they teach us something more.

They teach us how it is that we, too, can come to know the risen Jesus.'Let Jesus walk with you' they say to us. 'Ask him your questions.' And by the time you get home, you will understand. Luke is doing more here than recounting an important resurrection story: he is also setting down the pattern that the Early Church were to see repeated over and over again for three centuries before power and property changed their ways of operating to something we would recognize more easily today. Luke is showing us the pattern by which people come to faith, and central to the pattern is time spent walking with Jesus. As we do so, we come to know him. Revelation comes most freely when we take the time to walk.

There is convincing evidence that two factors were essential to the process by which the church grew in its first three centuries: the majority of converts began the journey of faith because someone they knew introduced them to the faith and the journey to conviction and conversion took time – weeks, months or even years. Conversion was rarely an instant event in the Early Church: it was viewed as a process that took time and was usually (though not always) 'topped off' by the public act of baptism. Whilst the dramatic events of Pentecost brought the Church to birth in a flurry of three thousand decisions, history shows that the disciple-making community very quickly developed a rhythm whereby Catechesis (coming to faith over a period of time through a learning journey, essentially an early Alpha course), became the norm. Even those who, like Paul, experienced a dramatic and sudden change followed this with a period of learning and growth. In his letter to the Galatians, he explains that he took three years out before he went back to Jerusalem to meet Peter and the disciples. What was Paul doing during these three years? He was walking with Jesus. And what was Jesus doing? Just as on the road to Emmaus, he was 'beginning with Moses and all the Prophets' . . . explaining 'what was said in all the Scriptures concerning himself' (Lk. 24:27). There was a period for Paul of getting to know Jesus; of building relationship and growing in faith. Piece by piece, he had to take all he had learned amongst the greatest Pharisees of his day and realign it to the reality of Jesus. Paul became the greatest Christian apologist of all history because he walked with Jesus.

RELATIONAL

Connecting with your Creator

Companionship is wonderful. Even more wonderful is realising who your closest companion is: God almighty, the Creator and sustainer of the universe, able to empower you to face anything that comes your way.

Bill Hybels[4]

There is something about sunbathing that tells us more about what prayer is like than any amount of religious jargon. You're not going to get a better tan by screwing up your eyes and concentrating. You simply have to be there where the light can get at you.

Rowan Williams[5]

The gospels insist that the invitation of Jesus to 'walk with me, work with me and watch what I do' was not limited to his early group of close friends: it was in fact his promise to the world. Writing of John's record of the resurrection of Jesus, Tom Wright sees this as the very centre of the message

Gradually we realise what is happening. The extraordinary, intimate, unique relationship which Jesus himself had enjoyed with the Father is now open to all his followers. John finally explains why and how this comes about, in the first of his resurrection chapters. The risen Jesus tells Mary Magdalene to go and say to 'my brothers', 'I am going up to my Father *and your Father*, to my God *and your God*' (Jn. 20:17). Jesus, as himself the fulfilment and goal of Israel's vocation to be God's son, his beloved one, now shares this status, and its benefits, with all his followers. God's intention for the end, to draw humans freely into intimate fellowship with himself, has come forward to meet us in Jesus of Nazareth.[6]

To his first followers, Jesus promised that the secrets of his 'unique Father-Son operation coming out of Father and Son intimacies and knowledge' would be revealed. He invited them to observe the closeness of his own relationship with the Father and promised that they, too, would be invited into such intimacy. But this offer was not only for those who walked in the physical presence of Jesus. No-one is going to change the world just by making Simon Peter happy. The open secret of the Christian faith, the unique miracle of the ministry of Christ is that this world-transforming Father-Son relationship is available to all. If the worldwide growth of Christianity were a huge, global Lego festival, then intimacy with God would be the little six dot rectangular block at the heart of it all. Intimacy is the very basis of this faith

Without doubt, Peter and the others realized this within days of the resurrection, and everything Jesus ever said to them took on new meaning. John, for example, remembered a strange conversation when Jesus warned his friends that he would soon leave them. 'But it is actually best for you that I go away', he said (Jn. 16:7).Why? Because by returning to the Father he could send his Spirit to them and he (the Spirit) could lead them into *all* truth. So to those to whom Jesus had said 'walk with me, work with me and watch what I do' he now says 'I am going away and it's better for you that I do.' In the same conversation Jesus says, again to his closest friends, 'There is so much more I want to tell you, but you can't bear it now' (Jn. 16:10).

Read those words again, but try to read them as members of the early disciple-making community. Peter and John are your heroes. They are the *apostles* (the word is spoken in hushed tones of awe and reverence) and the qualification for their apostleship is that they have been with Jesus. They, more than anyone, had the opportunity to walk, work and watch with Jesus. Surely they, more than anyone, would understand his secrets? But what did he himself tell them? And what did they themselves confess, when it came time to write the gospel records? *That there were things to be known about Jesus that could not be known by being with him – but would be revealed to those who received his Spirit.* They (the apostles) had no advantage that was not also given to us (the community of the Spirit). Whether I came to faith five minutes, five years or five centuries after the resurrection, I am offered exactly the same deal as Peter, John, Mary, James, Cleopas, Paul and Lydia. I am invited into a relationship of intimacy with Jesus and the Father, because since the resurrection that relationship is mediated not through the physical presence of the Son of Man (one place, one time) but through the dispersed ministry of the Holy Spirit (everywhere, all the time).

This astounding truth catapults the invitation of Matthew 11 from the dust and rocks of a Jerusalem hillside forward, into every place and time and situation anyone of us is in. To the techno-immersed child of the twenty-first century, phone in pocket, iPod in ear, Jesus says by the Spirit 'Walk with me.' To the lone flat-dweller crushed by sickness and old age and neglect and forced to live out whatever days remain in painful loneliness Jesus says by the Spirit 'Walk with me.' To the parent struggling to feed her child; the patient wrestling with the death-sentence of a positive test result; the underground pastor torn from his family and carried into exile; the middle manager wondering why a bigger house and a better car and a faster laptop haven't produced a deeper life . . . to each of these Jesus says by the Spirit 'Walk with me.'

Just as on the road to Emmaus, Jesus draws alongside all those who will welcome him; to share their journey; to hear their story and, in time, to tell them his. 'Walk with me', by the sending of the Spirit and in the shadow of the resurrection, becomes the universal invitation to *all* of intimacy with their Maker. And this intimacy is the basis of all else God offers to us. 'Leave empty things to empty-minded people', wrote Thomas à Kempis in *The Imitation of Christ*, 'and direct your thoughts to God's commands for you. Shut the door upon yourself and invite in Jesus your beloved.' Relationship is the foundation of our faith and, by definition, the most vital building block of prayer. This gives us the first principle of prayer, without which it is impossible to take even one step further in our journey

Prayer is founded on the building and maintaining of a relationship

As self-evident as this truth may seem, there is a great and tragic irony to it: it is almost certainly the least understood and least practised aspect of prayer in our churches.

Pagan petitions

Despite all the efforts our God has made since the very waking moments of our world to communicate this offer to us, we consistently misunderstand the centrality of relationship to prayer. There are a number of reasons for this and unless we deal with them, there is little point in trying to go further. In our experience, there are three misunderstandings that come up time and time again and keep many of us on the nursery slopes of prayer when God is calling us to ski a red run or two. Firstly, we misread God's intentions towards us and our world, secondly we misunderstand the purpose of prayer and thirdly we allow fear to live in rooms designed for trust. These three are clearly linked together and form the contours of an essentially pagan understanding of God (or *the gods*) that has held much of the world in primitive terror for most of history. And continues to do so. There is nothing inherent in skyscrapers, telephones and washing machines that guarantees that the people who live amongst them will not be victim to a primitive, pagan view of the divine. In fact, there maybe something in the design of all three that encourages such a view. It is not only in jungle clearings that the village elders won't move until they have consulted the idol in the corner of the room. Calling it the NASDAQ index doesn't make it any less a god.

Taking the broadest possible view of the human condition and our attempts to understand our Creator, it does seem that this view of the divine is a default setting in our thinking: a setting that the more developed spiritualities try to correct. In this setting, three things are true about the relationship between humanity and divinity

Firstly, humans stand before God – or the gods – as victims. The gods don't like us very much and will take every opportunity to do us harm. In the Christianized version of this myth, God is given a good reason not to like us: we have sinned and offended him. We are by nature in his bad books and it is his intention to distance himself from us, to look on us with disdain and from time to time to smite us just to remind us who's boss. The primary emotion of God or the gods towards us is anger and unless we do something to appease this emotion, it will end in tears for us.

Secondly, it follows that the primary purpose of prayer is to plead for mercy and if possible to arrange some kind of benefit system in place of the smiting. If we plead enough, surely this God or gods will decide to give in to us and bless our crops instead of striking them with lightning. It helps, in most systems of belief, to leave some kind of offering – whether a few grains of rice, a turtledove or a nicely calculated pre-tax tithe. After all, why would these capricious, angry gods let us off the hook if we don't pay them tribute? The proof that this pagan view has fully invaded our Christian understanding of prayer lies in the fact that so many of our prayers seem to consist of trying to persuade God to do something good that we assume he doesn't otherwise want to do. It never occurs to us that we would not tolerate this kind of relationship with our own children for one minute, yet we persist in treating God, at least some of the time, this way.

Thirdly, the result of this arrangement is that the primary attribute of our relationship with the divine will not be trust but fear. We can't have a relationship of trust because the gods are actually out to harm us unless paid off in full and we are out to talk them into de-smiting us at the lowest possible cost to ourselves. Like purchasers of a secondhand car, we want the best deal we can get but don't really trust those we are dealing with. Trust and fear are mutually exclusive and a relationship built on one cannot tolerate the other. We have to choose.

Our challenge as Christ-followers is that this view of the divine – built on the three pillars of the anger of the gods, prayer as appeasement and fear in place of trust – is entirely antithetical to the relationship with God offered by the one who invites us to walk, work and watch. No matter how prevalent this view of God may be in human cultures, it is a view that cannot remain if we are to grow to maturity in our relationship with the Father, Son and Spirit, revealed to us in our Scriptures. If we are to build an authentic life of Christian prayer, we are going to have to deal with this pagan worldview and ask ourselves just how the God revealed in Christ differs from the monster we fear. And this is foundational. No technique or practice of prayer will be effective for us unless built on the right relationship. It is the reality of Jesus, not our pagan imagination, that must provide for us our picture of God. 'The key, then, to loving God', writes Dallas Willard, 'is to see *Jesus*, to hold him before the mind with as much fullness and clarity as possible.'

The golden sceptre

And when we do take time to deeply know the Christ story, we find that it offers – in the face of the default, pagan view of the human-divine relationship – some stunning claims about God. Perhaps we need to spend time considering these claims before moving deeper in our experience of prayer.

Firstly, the revelation of Jesus suggests that the default attitude of God towards us is not anger but love. God's desire is to be intimate with us – his vision of a world

that works well is a garden in which he takes a walk
with us in the cool of the evening. The 'wrath' of God –
better understood as the grieving or suffering of God,
literally his *passion* – comes into play because of the great
tragedy of our rebellion. We are broken people, people
who need to be set-right, repaired and renewed and God
reaches out to do just that for us. Christ on the cross did
not *change* the attitude of God from one of anger to one
of suffering: he made visible to us the suffering of God
that had always been the fruit of our rebellion. The crucified God is our God, from all eternity and forever. His
desire is not to leave us in our brokenness so that he can
take advantage of the longed-for opportunity to smite
us. Rather, he longs to heal us so that intimacy can be
restored. If your picture of God says to you 'I can't bear
the sight of you – get your filthy body out of my presence' you will struggle to grow in prayer. If you can picture, rather, a God who extends his embrace towards
you, like the king holding out the golden sceptre of
mercy to Esther – a God who, for all your brokenness,
longs to hold you – you have begun to understand what
kind of soil a life of prayer will grow in. The primary
revelation of the life of Christ is that God is love. If this
revelation is not the basis on which we pray, in what
sense are our prayers *Christian* at all?

Secondly, the life of Jesus tells us that the solution to our
rebellion is not that we appease God with our offerings
and persuade him with our whining not to smite us: it is
that we accept that he has dealt quite differently with our
sin. The remarkable and world-changing message of grace
is that there has indeed been smiting: but he, not we, has
taken the blows. Write it on your heart and on your chest;
pin it to your doorway; scratch it in the sky: *because of Jesus
there is nothing I have done or could do or will do that prevents
me from receiving God's embrace*. Prayer is not appeasement

or persuasion, it is relationship. God does not say to us 'Make me your best offer', he says 'Let me get to know you.' Prayer is conversation. It is whatever it takes for two people who do not know each other well to get to know each other well. How do strangers become friends? How do those who have grown apart grow together? How do you get to know a long lost relative? How do adoptive parents become intimate with their new children? How do distant colleagues become a team? Whatever answers come to mind as you ponder these questions are aspects of prayer. Gather all your answers together and you will find that you are describing Christian prayer as well as it can be described. As long as you feel or fear that you must appease God before he will speak to you, you will spend your whole life on the doorstep of prayer and never step into the house. Are you leaning so heavily on the doorbell that you don't even hear God saying to you '*Come right in, I've been expecting you*'?

Thirdly, Jesus makes it clear to us that in place of our neo-pagan life of *fear* we are called to build a life of *trust*. Just a few moments before offering us his 'walk, work, watch' invitation, Jesus has himself been in prayer – and his words must have been overheard by those around him, because we are told exactly what he prayed

> O Father, Lord of heaven and earth, thank you for hiding these things from those who think themselves wise and clever, and for revealing it to the childlike. Yes, Father, it pleased you to do it this way (Mt. 11:25-26 NLT).

In Eugene Peterson's *The Message* these words become

> Thank you, Father, Lord of heaven and earth. You've concealed your ways from sophisticates and know-it-alls, but spelled them out clearly to ordinary people. Yes,

> Father, that's the way you like to work (Mt. 11:25-26 *The Message*).

Among the many implication of this appeal to a 'child-like' faith is that there must be an element of *trust* if this relationship is to work. The one thing children do that know-it-alls don't is trust. Where trust has not been established, even the best of motives will be misunderstood and the most generous offers of help refused. So with God: if your relationship is founded on fear and distrust, you will misunderstand every offer he makes. God is love perfected, and perfect love, as the Apostle John reminds us, 'expels all fear' (1 Jn. 4:18 NLT).

Fear is like excess baggage or contraband goods. You can hang on to it or you can see your life of prayer take off but you cannot do both. To grow in prayer is to grow in relationship with God – and to grow in relationship with God is to grow in trust. There is no other route.

Rain and fruit

There is a wonderful picture in Isaiah that illustrates not only God's desire that we should connect with him, but also just how often and how easily we misunderstand his intentions. In Isaiah 55, the prophet issues God's passionate invitation to all who are willing to enter, or perhaps re-enter, a relationship with him

> 'Is anyone thirsty? Come and drink—even if you have no money!
> Come, take your choice of wine or milk—it's all free!
> Why spend your money on food that does not give you strength?
> Why pay for food that does you no good?

Listen to me, and you will eat what is good.

You will enjoy the finest food.

Come to me with your ears wide open.

Listen, and you will find life.

I will make an everlasting covenant with you.

I will give you all the unfailing love I promised to David.

See how I used him to display my power among the peoples.

I made him a leader among the nations.

You also will command nations you do not know,

and peoples unknown to you will come running to obey,

because I, the LORD your God,

the Holy One of Israel, have made you glorious.'

Seek the LORD while you can find him.

Call on him now while he is near.

Let the wicked change their ways

and banish the very thought of doing wrong.

Let them turn to the LORD that he may have mercy on them.

Yes, turn to our God, for he will forgive generously (Is. 55:1–7 NLT).

What a beautiful picture of a God who longs for intimacy with his people; a God who offers abundance and fruitfulness; who longs to speak with us; who is generous and merciful and forgiving and close. What a sparkling contrast to the capricious, mean-spirited anger of the pagan gods.

But in verse 8 something strange happens and God speaks words through the prophet that have been used, generation upon generation, to speak not of his closeness to us but of his distance from us

'My thoughts are nothing like your thoughts', says the
LORD.
'And my ways are far beyond anything you could imag-
ine.
For just as the heavens are higher than the earth,
so my ways are higher than your ways
and my thoughts higher than your thoughts' (Isa. 55:8–9
NLT).

The God of abundance and intimacy is gone. The God
who wants to communicate with us is replaced by a god
we won't even begin to understand: a god who by his
very nature is alien to us, as remote and inaccessible as
the sky above the earth. 'You can look, but you can't
touch' says this god of distance and derision.'Don't even
think of having a relationship with me . . .' Or so we
think. Our default paganism rears its head and throws
this text at us to prove that God is inaccessible, that the
dream of intimacy with him was always false. He is a
Victorian father, disciplinarian and dismissive. And we
have seen and heard this verse quoted in just that sense:
explaining to young people why it is that God is so
strange and why they should get used to it and stop asking so many questions. God is an alien, after all: you
can't expect to understand him!

And so, lost in the tragedy of our pagan bias, we miss
one of the most beautiful images in Scripture of the God
who longs for intimacy with us. Because we stop reading. There's only room for a short extract on our desk
calendar. But if we would only read on, we would see
that this picture of coldness and distance, this alien God,
is the exact opposite of what the prophet is telling us.

The rain and snow come down from the heavens and
stay on the ground to water the earth. They cause the

grain to grow, producing seed for the farmer and bread for the hungry. It is the same with my word. I send it out, and it always produces fruit. It will accomplish all I want it to, and it will prosper everywhere I send it. You will live in joy and peace. The mountains and hills will burst into song, and the trees of the field will clap their hands! Where once there were thorns, cypress trees will grow. Where nettles grew, myrtles will sprout up. These events will bring great honour to the Lord's name; they will be an everlasting sign of his power and love (Is. 55:10–11 NLT).

As you read this beautiful picture of a rain-soaked land yielding its fruits, you realize that you have misread the preceding verses and misconstrued what they have to say to you about God. Yahweh is not saying 'The sky is separate from the earth: I am separate from you – get used to it.' He is in fact saying '*Even though* the sky is separate from the earth – distant and different, untouchable and unattainable – *it is still possible* for the earth and sky to live in a mutually joyous relationship of abundance and fruitfulness.' Why? Because the sky *pours out its goodness* on the earth in the form of rain and snow and the earth is fruitful in response. And so, God says, I will pour my word into you so that you can be fruitful.

This is a picture of human thriving, of men and women and children living in wondrous fruitfulness because God has poured himself into them: a spiritual ecosystem in which earth and Heaven unite in harvest celebration. It is a picture of intimacy because self-revelation, the very essence of what it means for God to speak his word to us, is the deepest act of intimacy we know. The bridegroom who says to his new wife, 'I am willing for you to know everything there is to know about me. I am willing to be fully known' is more deeply loved for his act of self-revealing. To 'open up' to another, to 'let them in' to the deepest parts of who you are is a far more permanent and meaningful act of intimacy than any act of physical passion. And Yahweh wants to remind his people that he is the God of self-revelation. He *wants* to be known by his people and he wants to know them: this is an invitation to intimacy.

Isaiah 55 does not reinforce the pagan view of a distant God who waits to be appeased. Rather, it offers a rare window into God's true desire: his longing for intimacy between Creator and creature. Centuries later, the apostle John, looking for words in which to contain the miracle of the coming of Christ, writes 'the word became flesh and dwelt among us.' In Christ, God's self-revelation becomes ultimate. He pours himself into humanity fully and finally. What greater sign could you ask for of God's desire for intimacy with you?

This is the starting point of our journey. Not only the affirmation that *all prayer is relationship* but the further assertion that this is a very particular kind of relationship: a relationship of trust. It exists because God wants it to. God is *for* me: committed to me. He has taken the initiative so that I can know that he wants this friendship. Learning to trust his intentions – throwing myself on his love with expectant abandon – is the first step towards the deepest life of prayer known to humanity.

Exercises

Prayer is relationship

Consider the elements that you think contribute to the healthy growth of a relationship: you might think, for instance, that *time* should be invested, not only doing things together but simply being together; you might suggest that *listening* is important, each person being truly heard by the other; you might want to say that complete *transparency* and *honesty* are essential. Make a list of the five or six most important elements. Now ask yourself: what is the place for this in my relationship with God?

Prayer is trust

Take some time to reflect on your walk with God over the past 12 to 24 months. Ask yourself where are the high spots where you have truly trusted God, and where are the low spots, where you have given way to fear? What made the difference? What can you do to see fear expelled? Try noting in a journal the things you have said or done that might be construed as being born out of fear – then, on another page, those things born of trust. Do you see a pattern in the difference between the two? Are there ways you can shift the balance from being the fearful you to being the trusting you?

The empty chair

Therapists sometimes use a technique of recreating a conversation you have had in the past with someone you love by asking you to talk to an empty chair, imagining that the person is there in front of you. Try doing the same for a while with God. Rather than praying to a God 'somewhere out there', imagine God on a chair beside you. What do you want to say?

Emmaus Road

If you have struggled in recent months to find time to pray, take a literal walk with God. If possible, walk somewhere where people will not think you are crazy for talking to yourself. Book some time: two hours; a morning; a whole day and talk with God as you walk. Shout at him if you have to; cry if you need to. Imagine him asking you 'So how is life going for you?' and 'How do you feel about that? and 'What would you ask me if nothing was considered off-limits?'

Table for two

A few years back in the Prayerhouse at Spring Harvest we created an intimate space for prayer by preparing a bistro table, laid up for two diners. There was a red-and-white checked table cloth; plates and cutlery; two wine glasses; a basket with bread rolls. Each person was invited to take a seat and dine with Jesus. Given such an invitation, what would you talk about?

Letters of love

If you sometimes find it hard to talk to God, *write* to him. Write 'Dear God . . .' and then say what you've been try-ing to say. Explain yourself; ask your questions; express your feelings. Sign off with love, then seal the letter and set it aside. Three months later, read it and ask, 'Did God answer?'

His Prayer – your prayer

Use the words of the Lord's Prayer (Mt. 6:9–14) as your framework for prayer. After each phrase, simply pray about the things that come to mind. If you run out of time, write some of the things down to pray about later. Come back daily to the list. Pray daily; ask daily; forgive daily; seek guidance daily. Let the categories sparked by the Lord's Prayer become the categories in which you pray: use the filing cabinet Jesus designed for you because he knew you would need one . . .

Prayer

Lord, let all that I am
Respond to all you are.
In our response
Jesus you are here.
You join us, human as we are,
In our praise of the Father.
As we put our trust in him;
As we remind ourselves of who he is;
You are here,
Showing us the perfect character of God.
Lord, let all that I am
Respond to all you are.

All that you are:
God of the broken and the weary;
Friend of the fatherless; humble king;
Hope in hopeless places;
Light where darkness reigns;
Freedom from every captivity;
Balm to every wound.
Lord, let all that I am
Respond to all you are.

All that I am.
My strength and my weakness.
My wisdom and my foolishness
My joy and my sadness
My head and my heart
My hands and my feet
Lord, let all that I am
Respond to all you are.

Chrissie Kelly

Blessing: The door

May he who opens doors
no man can shut
be your door-keeper.
May he who drives his very kingdom
to your doorstep,
who dares you
to dive into your dreams,
be your deliverer.

May he who never slams the door
on sympathy,
nor hinders wholeness,
who never turns the lock on love:
the sentry at the entry-way of mercy,
who thrives
at the threshold of kindness,
be your key-holder.

May he who stays behind closed doors
to seek you;
who calls you to closeness,
and invites you to intimacy:
who sings in secret rooms and quiet streams
find your embrace.

May he who knocks
and won't stop knocking,
who leans with all his weight
to wait for you
hear your steps coming,
your voice of greeting,
the latch loosening,
your rusted hinges

opening:
may his eyes find yours,
a welcome visitor.

And may he
walk you
to the narrow door,
the door for the sheep,
to the open door of Heaven:
and bring you through

Gerard Kelly

RHYTHMIC

Earthed in the everyday

I am challenged by the idea of entering into the joy of Sabbath as a glimpse of eternity. Taking the Sabbath seriously affects the rhythm and focus of my whole life, not just one day a week.

Christine Sine[7]

The real radicals aren't quoting Che Guevara or listening to Rage Against the Machine on their iPods. The true revolutionaries are learning to pray.

Wilson Hartgrove[8]

Impressionism was one of the most significant movements in Western art history. Covering the closing years of the nineteenth century, it focused mainly, though not exclusively, on France and brought breakthroughs in the theory and practice of painting that were foundational to all that followed in the twentieth century. Paintings by Monet and Renoir, as well as Van Gogh, Cezanne, Degas, Gauguin and Pissarro (who are usually called Post-Impressionists) remain some of the most valuable and valued works of art in the world today. The Impressionist period was a time of great innovation and experiment, particularly in the use of colour. The artists involved continually reviewed the way it was used and experimented in particular with the power of contrast.

Earlier artists had known instinctively how to use strong colours, but in the late nineteenth century, two parallel developments made it possible for such work to be both systematic and intentional. In the field of colour theory, scientists carrying out experiments with light came to understand as never before how colours work. A number of books and articles were published identifying exactly which colours served best as opposites to each other. Alongside these developments, there was significant growth in the availability of pigments, discovered both through global trading and chemical experiment. With an ever-expanding palette, the pioneers of what would become modern art were able to harness colour in new ways. In the course of their innovations, they proved a little-known truth about the human eye: that if two closely related colours are placed next to each other, there is a certain distance at which the eye and the brain will conspire to merge them. The artist may be aiming for subtlety, but what they get is sludge.

When 'complementary colours' are placed close together though – by which they mean paired opposites – each will retain its luminosity and tone over a much greater distance. Impressionist works are filled with such contrasts – an orange boat drifting on a deep blue river, a green vase against red walls. In 1888, Claude Monet said, 'Colour owes its brightness to force of contrast rather than to its inherent qualities . . . primary colours look brighter when they are brought into contrast with their complementaries.'[9] Monet's 1872 painting *Regatta at Argenteuil* uses this theory to the full: 'the blue water is embellished with strong orange; the red-roofed house sits amongst green foliage; and violet figures and shadows stand against the creamy yellow sails.'[10] The later styles of Van Gogh and Gauguin would take this even further, giving up on naturalism altogether to use colours in new ways and lay foundations for the later schools of Expressionist, Cubist and Abstract art.

It seems strange to us now that this notion of the complementarity of colours was not fully understood earlier. Artists knew how to use bright colours – Titian is the all-time master – but they didn't know that they could be made brighter simply by placing them next to their complement. In the juxtaposition of opposites, each party gains identity and strength. And what is true of colour may well be true of our lives: a rhythm of contrasting and complementary activities is healthier and more fulfilling than an uninterrupted commitment to one activity. This is a feature of the natural world. We live in the contrasts of night and day; summer and winter, earth and sky; hills and valleys. Our world is full of opposites that complete one another. The oasis is beautiful because it is found in the desert. Sleep is a blessing in the midst of an active life. Holidays renew and refresh us because they interrupt our working patterns. We love travelling because we have a home that we love to return to. The suggestion that contrasts bring definition and strength is not restricted to colour theory: it seems to be part of the created order of things. *Contrast* makes the world go round.

Rhythm and rest

In the Hebrew Bible – passed on to us in the Old Testament – this rhythm of contrasts and distinctions is presented as a foundational aspect of our world and is called Sabbath. It is introduced at the very outset, in the Garden of Eden. After a series of separations – earth and sky, sun and moon, night and day, sea and land, man and woman – God enters into his own separation by 'resting' from his 'work': and the pattern of Sabbath is born. Because we connect the word Sabbath so much with our view of Saturday or Sunday and with the long list of restrictions that both Jews and Christians have placed around these days, we miss the deeper meaning of the word. It is not essentially about a day, nor about rules and restrictions: it is about rhythm, the contrasts of our lives giving richness to our experience. Like yellow set against blue for emphasis, the rest of Sabbath is set against activity and work to illustrate its worth. A satisfying life, to the Hebrew, has strong, contrasting colours.

The significance of God's work-and-Sabbath rhythm is caught by Walter Brueggemann in his wonderful description of the world's first week

> The Bible starts out with a liturgy of abundance. Genesis 1 is a song of praise for God's generosity. It tells how well the world is ordered. It keeps saying, 'It is good, it is good, it is good, it is very good.' It declares that God blesses – that is, endows with vitality – the plants and the animals and the fish and the birds and humankind. And it pictures the creator as saying, 'Be fruitful and multiply.' In an orgy of fruitfulness, everything in its kind is to multiply the overflowing goodness that pours from God's creator spirit. And as you know, the creation ends in Sabbath. God is so overrun with fruitfulness that God says, 'I've got to take a break from all this. I've got to get out of the office.'[11]

Brueggemann's extravagant words point to the central reality of the meaning of Sabbath: rest is meaningful because it contrasts with labour; contemplation has meaning in contrast to action; 'worship' becomes powerful when it interrupts ordinary work. Prayer is meaningful precisely because it sits alongside and interrupts the other aspects of our lives. As Gordon Macdonald wrote in *Ordering Your Private World*, 'Does God indeed need to rest? Of course not! But did God choose to rest? Yes. Why? Because God subjected creation to a rhythm of rest and work that He revealed by observing the rhythm Himself, as a precedent for everyone else.'[12]

The essence of Sabbath is not religion but rhythm. This is the same claim Christine Sine makes in her assessment of Jesus' own timestyle. Looking at how Jesus prioritized his time, she says, 'I came to the conclusion that there were three rhythms that he balanced in his life – the rhythm between the spiritual and the secular, between work and rest and between community and solitude.'[13]

A thread through fabric

The idea of Sabbath is presented in Genesis as a creational reality; in Exodus and Deuteronomy as a commandment to do with worship and community and in the life of Jesus as a personal commitment. In each of these Sabbath represents both rest and rhythm.

Rest, because it calls us to give balanced attention to our different needs – the physical and emotional as well as the social and spiritual. Work is important to our thriving, but so is recreation. God calls us to enjoy Sabbath rest as a regular part of our experience.

Rhythm, because prayer and worship – intentionality in our relationship with God – have their rightful place as a thread woven through our other activities. The rhythmic nature of created life ensures that even as we give attention to the many tasks and relationships that confront us, we also give attention to our life with God. The life of faith and prayer is intended, in this way, to be threaded through our everyday activities.

This is why Jesus said that 'The Sabbath was made to benefit people, and not people to benefit the Sabbath' (Mk. 2:27 NLT). Rest and rhythm are not requirements God lays upon us but gifts he has created for us. A view of prayer that is Sabbath-driven will look for worship and surrender and hearing the voice of God as activities that run like a river through the landscape of our lives: not restricted to times of public worship but flowing through all our engagements, dancing and weaving through our days. The spiritual life is not a life of escape from everyday realities: it is a life in which those same realities are infused with prayer and the presence of God. Like a thread running through fabric, prayer can flow through our days: here spoken, there silent; here visible, there hidden; here the focus of our thinking, there the background of our living. Sabbath in its true sense does not teach us to have a pristine, religious part of our lives, one-seventh wide, into which we pour all our efforts at spirituality and prayer. Rather, it teaches us to 'observe' the 'pause moments' that will carry prayer into every moment.

> A spiritual practice is anything that connects us to God – a thought about the cleansing power of the Spirit as we have our shower, a revelation about the wonder of God as we look at a flower, an encounter with God reflected in the face of a stranger or the discipline of God administered through the voice of a friend are all spiritual practices that we both need to acknowledge and deliberately look for.[14]

This broader view of Sabbath was not restricted, for the Hebrew community, to the structure of the week: thinking about what to do (or not) on Saturday. There were also rhythms of the year – festivals that reflected the passing of the seasons but also marked the events by which Yahweh had revealed himself to his people. Jack Hayford points out that God's law is built on a calendar that has a cycle of worship at its heart: 'Worship is over and above all in the calendar the Lord outlines for the newly enfranchised society of former slaves. It was built upon weekly Sabbaths of worship, monthly new moons of worship and seasonal feasts of celebrative worship.'[15]

There were longer economic cycles of seven years and fifty years – the Sabbath year and the Jubilee year – by which the principles of rest and restoration were applied to the whole nation and even to the earth. When land is allowed to rest for a full year; when unpaid debts are cancelled and property returned to its hereditary owners; when slaves are freed across a nation, these are signs that the rhythms of rest are being taken seriously. The intention of Sabbath is not to ensure that we are miserable at least one day a week, it is to remind us to balance our activities with periods of rest and prayer. No success without Sabbath; no steaming ahead without stopping to rest. The aim is for balance and rhythm and for threads of God's peace that flow into every part of our lives. In a very deep sense these rules call us to remember who God is and who we are. The laws of Sabbath and Jubilee reminded the Hebrew people that the land was not theirs but God's: that *property* was a temporary arrangement that made fruitfulness possible, not a permanent right. Even slaves, who were in every other way owned by their masters, were given the right of Sabbath to be reminded that they were ultimately in the hands of God. The land, the animals and the people were given rhythms of rest so that they could *enter in* once again – and over and over again – to the rest into which they were born as creatures of God. And if an ancient, agricultural people needed such rhythms, how much more do we need to rediscover them?

To take seriously God's Sabbath call as we grow in the life of prayer will mean a willingness to re-examine the rhythms of our lives. What can we do that will weave a pattern of prayer into each day? How do our weekly plans allow for genuine Sabbath? As we look at the year ahead, have we made provision for times of retreat? What about a seventh-year commitment? (this is where we get the term *sabbatical* from, though the practice is limited to a very small and privileged range of occupations.) Is there some way that we can reflect this principle in our life-planning?

The open window

These questions will make a difference to our growth in prayer for two vital reasons. Firstly every choice to live a more biblically-shaped lifestyle will draw us closer to the God who calls us to Sabbath rest with him. Secondly it is these patterns of work and rest; activity and contemplation that give us the opportunity to engage in prayer at all. We can choose to focus our Sabbath times – whether daily, weekly or annually – on growing in prayer. The times we step aside from our regular activities can be when we seek God. This doesn't mean frantic, passionate prayer in every pause moment: but weaving the intentionality of our Godward relationship into our lives. When a couple keep 'date nights' well into the later years of their marriage, they do so because they know that without this intentional scheduling, the health of their relationship will take a backseat to more seemingly urgent priorities. Intimacy will be lost. We don't practise Sabbath rhythms as a point-scoring exercise in a parlour game called 'Religion.' We practise Sabbath and seek rhythms of prayer in the midst of our everyday lives to reflect the intentionality of our relationship with God: because in the spiritual, just as in the relational, we need our date nights.

Anatoly Emmanuilovich Levitin was a Russian dissident who was frequently in conflict with the authorities for his religious and political views. Even as an old man, he experienced imprisonment. During these times he sought to maintain the same rhythm of prayer and worship that had marked his life as a free man. And the practice – the commitment to living out a God-focussed rhythm of life in even the most discouraging of places – became a lifeline

> The basis of my life is the Orthodox liturgy (I do not, of course, deny other forms). Therefore, while in prison I attended the liturgy every day in my imagination. At 8 am I would begin walking around my cell, repeating to myself the words of the liturgy. At that moment I felt myself inseparably linked with the whole Christian world and then, standing before the face of the Lord and feeling almost physically his wounded and bleeding body, I would begin praying in my own words . . . The prison walls moved apart and the whole universe became my residence, visible and invisible, the universe for which that wounded, pierced body offered itself as a sacrifice . . . Not only my prayer, but much more the prayer of many faithful Christians helped me. I felt it continually. It worked from a distance, lifting me up as though on wings, giving me living water and the bread of life, peace of soul, rest and love.[16]

Here the rhythm of prayer makes a difference to the place of oppression: a daily period of Sabbath interrupts the pattern of solitude, fear and frustration, bringing an explosion of joy. Like Daniel praying three times daily at his open window, Levitin discovered that his heart could be in Jerusalem even when his body was in Babylon. These two pilgrims' passage through the valley of weeping made it a place of springs (Ps. 84:6). They made more of a dent on the Universe than it made on them and their grasp on the life of prayer meant that their environments echoed with their joy. Can we do the same? Can our ordinary become extraordinary through prayer? Scripture says yes. History affirms it and experience, even today, agrees.

When the Walls

When the walls
of Babylon are closing in
and Jerusalem
is a dim
and distant dream,
shut the door,
open a window
and pray.

When narrowness of vision
smothers hope
and stifles your every ambition,
shut the door,
open a window
and pray.

When you need to find your focus
in a free and far horizon
and to see beyond the furniture
that frames you,
shut the door,
open a window
and pray.

When darkness encroaches
and shadows fight with sight
and you crave the comfort of light,
shut the door,
open a window
and pray.

When the presence of God is a misted memory
and the promises of God are slow in coming

and the purposes of God are buried in the fields of your
anxiety,
when you are stuck,
stagnated,
struggling,
without hope
and without help in the world,
shut the door
in the presence of your Father,
open a window
to the promise of your Redeemer
and pray
to the one who loves and lives
for you
and longs to help you
more than you can ever know.

Gerard Kelly[17]

Three battles

The 'Sabbath rhythms' of our lives, whether worked out
in daily, weekly, monthly, annually or life-long patterns,
are the *containers* in which prayer will be made effective
to us. Like campers gathering at the communal tap, we
come armed with bottles and jugs, to carry back to our
pitch the precious water that we need. To commit to pray
each morning; to establish a three-times-a-day pattern; to
set aside a day each week for focused prayer; to plan
times of retreat through the seasons: these activities create structures into which the benefits of prayer will flow.
It's not the container that matters, it's the water – but
without the container, the water cannot reach us. From
the very beginning spiritual seekers have understood

that without intentionality, there is no growth in prayer, and intentionality is strongly linked to time. If love is spelt T I M E, so is prayer.

The battle for time, as we saw already in the example of Jesus, will tend to be fought on three fronts: in the rhythm between the spiritual and the secular, between work and rest and between community and solitude.[18]

Spiritual and secular

One of the corrections that many believers have brought to their lives in recent years is to move away from an attitude of *dualism* in which 'spiritual' activities are valued and 'secular' tasks ignored. This is a very important correction,which helps people to come to a wider, deeper and richer view of the mission of God in the world. But there is a danger that in emphasizing God's interest in the whole of life, we will lose altogether our commitment to spiritual practices. Like the physical and the emotional, the spiritual is part of who we are: it is a way of being human and it has a rightful place in the pattern of our lives. Like Jesus, we need to identify the *spaces* and *times* in which we will give attention to it. We will face many tasks in the secular aspects of our lives and God's desire for us is that we should embrace those tasks wholeheartedly. There is nothing holy about running from responsibility and nothing unholy about an honest day's work. But we face many tasks, too, in the spiritual domain and we can embrace them just as wholeheartedly. Our calling is to be fully present to the task God has given us – to practise what Jean Pierre de Caussade called 'the Sacrament of the present moment'[19] – and then to ensure that the tasks that fill our days are rhythmically divided between emotional, physical and spiritual pursuits.

Work and rest

Athletics trainers know that the best fruits do not come from sustained and uninterrupted training, but from a creative pattern of effort and rest: now pressing the muscles into service, now letting them relax. Sabbath is a pattern of rest that gives meaning to our patterns of work. It includes sleep and recreation, but it also includes quiet rest in God's presence when prayer is not working through our shopping list but the gentle joy of being silent in the presence of love. An Orthodox priest once told of an old man who came each day to the church to sit, always in silence and for sustained periods in the day. Curious, the priest asked what he was doing. 'Praying' the man said. 'And what kinds of things do you say to God?' the fascinated priest asked. 'Oh, nothing', the man replied, 'I just listen.' Thinking he was about to strike gold, the priest asked, 'And what does God say to you?' 'Oh, nothing' was the man's serene reply. 'He just listens.' Prayer is not just transferring our busy-ness from one sphere to the other: it is not badgering God. Rather, it is founded on resting in God and the interwoven pattern of work and rest is as much to do with prayer as with any other activity.

Community and solitude

There is without doubt a call to community for followers of Christ. Much that we are asked to do, we are asked to do *together* and the rediscovery of community is one of the marks of the Holy Spirit's renewing of the church. But there is also a call to *solitude* and this is less fluently understood in contemporary churches. Eastern and New Age practices, in fact, are far better at feeding the individual in solitude than much contemporary

Christian spirituality. But there is a dimension to prayer in which I am and must remain alone. Deep calls to deep as my heart hears the voice of my Creator and there are things he has to say to me that are for my ears only. There are battles to be fought, issues to be faced and joys to be experienced that are firmly in the realm of 'God and me.' But clearly we are not all called to live the life of a hermit and it is not an act of holiness, by definition, to separate myself from others. What is needed is rhythm, a dance that takes us from deep solitude to heartfelt community; from moments when in silence we confront the Lover of our souls to moments of fully attentive, intentional engagement with others. The beauty is in the rhythm, in the contrasting colours of solitude and community. Like a ballet, the aching elegance of the pas-de-deux is offset by the spinning glory of the full company. This is the rhythm of the life of Jesus and we would do well to learn from it.

Bashed and blessed

What can you do to ensure that the bright colours of your day-to-day 'secular' activities are shot through with the deeper hues of your spiritual life? How can you ensure that your 'for God' actions set into a 'with God' life? How will you foster a true solitude that feeds your soul and better equips you, when in the company of others, to be a course of life and hope? In all these things you will find health and strength in rhythm: the silence that makes sense of sound; the aloneness that makes togetherness possible; the stillness that gives meaning to movement.

> Prayer, what is it?
> It all begins in the heart, in relationship,

and needs to flow through the heart
so often broken and fragile.
Prayer heals and transforms
as well as strengthens and renews.
It's a lifeline,
it's a life-long journey with the Father, Son and Holy
    Spirit.
It's the coming that enables the going to happen;
It's the breathing in in order to be able to breathe out;
It's the 'make me' plea to be more Christlike,
The opportunity to ask for all that we need.
It's a channel for God's peace to flow
into our chaotic and often disturbed lives,
It offers the possibility for perfect intimacy and closeness
    with our Creator,
reconciliation with our Maker.
It is a powerhouse, it is our source.

Chrissie Kelly

We love these words of our good friend Ajith Fernando,
who explains why a rhythm of prayer and action is
essential to the lives of his teams in Youth for Christ, Sri
Lanka

> I tell our staff that Christian ministers are people who get
> their strength from God, go into the world and get
> bashed around. Then we come back, get our strength
> from God, go back into the world, get bashed around.
> And that is our life. We go, get bashed, get strength, go,
> get bashed, get strength. And we can take on strength in
> this way.[20]

Seeking to live out the rhythms of prayer evident in the
life of Jesus, many people drawn into new movements

of prayer in recent years have felt called to establish quite formal patterns of prayer. The 24/7 movement has given birth to new intentional communities called 'Boiler Rooms', inspired by monastic history. One of their key aims is to be 'a *prayerful* community, practising a daily rhythm of which includes intercession, contemplation and Christian worship.'[21] Inspiration comes both from Scripture and from Christian history. Daniel's 'three-times-a-day' life of prayer was also believed to be the pattern established in the temple at Jerusalem, with formal prayers taking place at 9:00am, noon and dusk. The Benedictine Rule, practised since the fifth century AD, lays out a vigorous schedule of daily prayer including vigils through the middle of the night, matins before dawn, vespers just before the setting of the sun and compline in the late evening. In addition, the Boiler Rooms look for a regular rhythm of more focused seasons of prayer, such as one week in six committed to prayer 24/7. Similar 'new monastic' communities are emerging in many Western cultures, often in high-pressure urban environments. They vary in their expressions but tend to draw inspiration in similar ways from the traditions of the monastic life, particularly in three areas: to explore what it means to live in community; to be committed to the poor and disadvantaged so as to offer an embrace to *all*; and to find some pattern by which prayer can be worked out in the everyday.

These are all ways of exploring 'Sabbath' in its true, rhythmic sense without falling prey to the 'Bible-black' traditions of social legalism. Ironically, it is many of the looser church networks – those moving away from 'Sunday worship' as the heart of the church community – that are most exploring daily and seasonal prayer rhythms. The core issue is not Sunday, but Sabbath. Is there a rhythm by which the daily realities of our lives –

our secular, communal, working lives can be interlaced with prayer and thereby soaked with God's presence? We will not grow much past our infancy in prayer unless we can find such rhythms.

Exercises

Liminal prayer: coming apart at the seams

If someone asked you how your life was going and you answered 'I'm coming apart at the seams', it would probably not be received as good news. But there is a sense in which it could be the best news ever. 'Coming apart' is an old-fashioned term for the life of prayer. It means turning aside from our regular activities to focus on our life with God, setting our eyes on our Creator. You don't have to go to church to come apart. You can come apart anywhere. You can fill your day with moments of coming apart. But when are the moments most given to coming apart to be with God? The answer is often in the joining places. The moments between waking and sleeping, between home and work; the pause between appointments. These are liminal moments: stages between one state and the next and they most offer the chance of private thoughts in an otherwise public day. What can you do to 'come apart with God' in these moments? What prayers are appropriate to such snatched bursts of intimacy?

> On your bus-ride to work, think about how a crowded bus can be turned into a place of prayer. Most people these days are an 'absent presence' already, lost in a book, on their iPod or fiddling with their phone. How can you carry resources that will turn these moments to

prayer? What about guided prayers on MP3, or a prayer framework on a simple card you can carry?

Think about having a conversation with God when driving. 'Call' God on your mobile and talk to him hands-free. Consider making every traffic light you meet a place of prayer.

At your school or office, consider whether there is a place you can easily retire to even for a few moments: perhaps a roof-top space or an unused room, perhaps a lobby area that isn't crowded. Smokers have become expert at finding such places to escape the banning of their habit: why not pray-ers?

Once you have identified some of the seams in your life that you can convert to prayer moments, commit to using them with regularity: *every* traffic light; two seconds before *each* meeting; the same bus ride *every* day. The regularity of the commitment will help you to remember, but it will also make your prayer rhythmic, sewing a pattern of prayer into the fabric of your day. Come apart at the seams and see what a difference it might make to your days. What about offering a silent prayer every time you cross a boundary or threshold?

Pause, rewind, play

There is also great scope for creating 'pause moments' in the day and habitually turning them to prayer. These are micro-moments that pepper our experience and often go unnoticed. The time that it takes to boil a kettle, to take a shower . . . In the Celtic tradition each of these would have its own prayer. We still have records of prayers to go along with lighting the fire, milking the cow or washing the face. Perhaps we could create such prayers. A prayer for the fire of God's Spirit to burn strong in us as we are watching the kettle come to the boil; a prayer for inner cleansing and renewal as we shower; a prayer to the Trinity as you wash your face, scooping the water three times. Think about the 'pause moments' that most regularly occur in your days and which of them could most easily be turned to prayer.

Spot the dot

Many years ago a team came together to resource prayer for a major UK event at which Billy Graham was speaking. They wanted a way to remind their supporters to pray for the people involved, leading up to the event. Their solution was to ask each praying person to put a small red dot – the kind of sticker that you can easily buy at an office supplier – on the face of their watch. The idea was to provide a memory-jogger so that every time the pray-er looked at their watch, they were reminded to pray.

The fishbowl of faith

We have a friend in London who used to feel guilty about all the people he promised to pray for, but didn't. He realized that he wanted to pray for so many people that to do so every day was impractical. The people at the top of the list would get loads of prayer, the people lower down none: and he wasn't organized enough to figure out a timetable. He came up with an ingenious if unusual solution. He found an empty fishbowl at home and, whenever he committed to pray for someone, he wrote their names on a slip of paper and folded it into the bowl. Each morning he would close his eyes, rummage around and pull out one slip and that person would get the full attention of his prayers that day. He was reckoning that by the law of averages (or, if you're a Calvinist, by the sovereignty of God) each person would get prayed for at least a few times a year. We know that he carried through on his commitment to this system, because he once said 'God must be doing something significant in your lives right now, because you popped out of my fishbowl three times in the past two weeks!' An unexpected spin-off of this system was that he actually had *fun* praying.

Thanktank

We can all learn to say thank you more. The German mystic Meister Eckhart taught that 'If the only prayer you said in your whole life was, 'Thank you' that would suffice'[22] and we don't say thank you enough. Some people have managed to hang onto the practice of saying grace before meals and what for many used to be a legalistic, empty gesture has become a rare island of gratitude in an ungrateful world. Some have the practice, in the last moment before sleep, of simply thanking God for the warmth, safety and comfort of a bed and for the home that allows a family to rest in peace. Some have learned in their first waking moments to pause and thank God for the day. The truth is that if we were to exhaustively note every blessing for which we might legitimately say thank you, there would be enough for every waking breath. When Jesus took bread in his own hands and the crumbs from it fell to the table, he urged us every time we do the same to remember him. Was he talking about a once-a-year Passover Meal, or a once-a-month or once-a-week Communion or Eucharist, or was he perhaps saying something simpler? *'Every time you see bread, think of me. Every time you break it, remember me.'* Sew gratitude and prayer into the very fabric of your day and you will find that fabric transformed.

Spiritual practices help us to see the ordinary with new eyes, to convert our everyday experiences into worship. Imagine a neighbourhood in which little or no rain has fallen for years. The grass is pale and yellowing; there is dust everywhere. But an arrangement has been made to pipe water to a local swimming pool and once a week you are allowed to jump in. Your weekly dip is essential to your comfort and survival. Now imagine that policies change and instead of being pumped into the pool, those same gallons of water are diverted: to homes and businesses and sprinkler systems right across the community. You are soaked in water every day. The grass recovers its colour and strength. The dust goes. A sense of life and health returns to the community. Both pictures show the same water, but in one image it is concentrated and in the other it is dispersed. This goes some way to illustrating the way we have misunderstood Sabbath. We have sought to *concentrate* our spirituality in one part of our lives, perhaps on one day of the week, rather than *dispersing* the rhythms of God through our days. We have collected the refreshment of God in a pool instead of pumping it into a sprinkler system. And we are surprised that we spend most of our time dry.

The beauty of God's supply, the abundant miracle of his grace, is that he has water enough for pools *and* sprinklers. Sabbath understood as one day in seven is part of the package, and the gathering of God's people is part of the joy. There is water, too, for the sprinkler systems and God's desire is that your life be *soaked* with his presence, everyday, everywhere you go – the contemplation of God-laced through your experience. Prayer is not an activity carried out in churches, it is an activity carried *into* every part of your life. God's presence is portable. Prayer is a plug-and-play programme.

Reflection

This meditation, called 'Pray without ceasing', was written by Christine Sine in the approach to Christmas 2007 and reflects on the challenges of prayer in the everyday.

As we move toward Advent I have been thinking a lot about what it means to pray without ceasing – a concept that I have always struggled with and at times felt guilty about. For most of my Christian life I have thought of prayer as constant intercession, something that gets both exhausting and draining – and that kind of prayer is impossible to do 'without ceasing.'

In recent years I have come to another understanding of prayer. To pray without ceasing means to open our eyes, our ears and our hearts so that we can see the prayers that are already hidden deep within every act of life

- the prayers of thankfulness for God's provision
- the prayers of praise when we catch a glimpse of God in the beauty of creation
- the prayers of confession when something strikes deep into our souls and reveals our hidden sins
- prayers of lament when we do not understand the pain and anguish of our friends
- prayers of intercession when we grieve over the horrors we read about in the newspaper

Every mundane act of life can be a revelation of our God if our ears are open to hear the whisper of the

Spirit who is present in every part of life and in every moment of the day and if our eyes are open to see the wonder of a God who is behind us, before us and inside us. What do we hear and see?

- the whisper of a guiding father who leads and instructs us in the ways we should go
- the whisper of a compassionate, caring mother whose heart aches for us in the midst of our pain
- the whisper of a God who desires the intimacy and closeness of a lover.[23]

Blessing

This blessing was written for Watershed Church in Charlotte, North Carolina[24] for Mothers' Day in 2008. The church wanted to particularly honour the lives of single mothers.

> When the day is longer
> Than the energy you have for it,
> And the tasks you face outlast you ten times over:
> May the rest and restoration God
> Be your Restorer.
>
> When the mouths you feed,
> And the minds you mould,
> And the hearts whose hopes you hold as guarantor
> Engulf you:
> When the eyes whose desperation dents your dreams
> Look at and through you
> May God who sees the needs of all who seek him
> Be your shelter.
>
> When you dread that you don't do enough,
> And hate that you don't have enough;
> When you know that you don't know enough,
> And fear that you won't be enough;
> When all you can be sure of,
> Is that there's something you'll need more of:
> May God, who is beyond enough
> Be your enough.
>
> May he who is always around you
> Surround you
> May he who has gone before you
> Be for you

May he who is beneath and above you
Love you
May he who invisibly holds you
Enfold you

May you know
Beyond the boundaries of knowing
And feel
Beyond the frailty of your feelings
That you are loved
And may he who, seen or unseen, is your kinsman
Be your Redeemer.

Gerard Kelly

Work

From the earliest memories of my childhood, 'home' was a place filled with the noises of my father's work. When I was playing in the yard outside his workshop, or sitting with the other children and the women, they were always there in the background: my father, his brothers and my cousins. There were comings and goings: deliveries, collections, customers come to haggle and dispute and seek better work at a lower cost (though they always accepted my father's price in the end, because they knew that he was fair and that the work could not be bettered). My uncles and cousins would go off to work elsewhere, to deliver beams and frames to a site or price up a new job, but my father would always stay in the workshop. My family's reputation was guaranteed by his personal oversight of the work. Not one piece of wood left our home that he himself had not touched.

Sometimes, when he was alone in the workshop, I would try to get closer, to watch him through the open doorway. I knew I could not cross the threshold: this I had learned before I knew how to recognize a scorpion or stay clear of the rear end of a donkey. The workshop was not a place for children. There were tools and dangers and there was work to be done. Even my mother, though this rule did not apply to her, stayed away. The day we went in together to tidy my dead father's tools was the first time I had ever seen her in that hallowed place.

I watched my father from a distance, waiting for the moments when the sun would send shafts of light through the window to illuminate the movements of his hands over the wood.

When I was seven years old, something changed. My father began, from time to time, to catch my eye as I watched and even to smile at me as he worked. The exclusion zone around the workshop's door seemed to be shrinking and I dared to move a little closer. And then a day came when he spoke the most wonderful words. Putting down the tools he had been working with, he looked directly at me and said 'Do you want to help?'

I hesitated, unsure if I had heard him well, but he kept eye contact and beckoned for me to cross the threshold of his world.

'One day this will be your work, not mine', he said, 'It's time you began your learning.'

I stepped forward nervously, as he returned to his work. He fell into a pattern of working for a few moments, then stopping to explain what he was doing, telling me the names of the tools and what they were for. He was finishing a short beam that he told me would serve as a lintel, to anchor the frame of a doorway. But this was no ordinary doorway – it would stand in the new home of Matthias the priest, one of the richest and most important men in our town. This would be a lintel people talked about.

He was working the wood, smoothing it and from time to time pouring oil onto its surface and rubbing it in. Then he urged me to come closer still. Taking a piece of untreated wood from the floor, he put it onto the work table beside the lintel he had been working on.

'I want to show you something', he said. 'Close your eyes.'

I shut my eyes tight and sensed his body moving closer to mine. He took my hands in his and placed them on the wood he had lifted from the floor.

'Feel this', he said. 'Do you feel how it is rough, unworked?'

I moved my fingers carefully, wary of splinters. I nodded.

'Now feel this', he said, lifting my hands onto the lintel he had been finishing. 'Do you feel the difference?'

I did. There was a silky residue of the oil – but even without this, the beam was smooth to the touch and warm. I trailed my hands across the contours of the wood, feeling *every tiny swirl and groove. It was like mapping the world, following the hills and valleys, finding the pathways. But this was a world that had been washed by rain and shaped by wind until every contour surrendered smoothly to the next. It was as if the wood had a fingerprint – the markings were as subtle and as unique. Someone would be paying a high price for the care and effort my father had put into preparing this beam: years from now, decades even, they would still be grateful for his work.*

'It's not enough to see the difference', my father said. 'I want you to feel it. You must learn to read the wood: to know it so well that you alone can say when it is finished. And when you've grown used to feeling it in your fingers, you will feel it in your heart. Only then can you be sure that the work you do is as good as it can possibly be.'

And in that moment my education began. I spent every hour I could beside my father and he began to trust me with simple tasks – choosing the raw beam that would form the next lintel, measuring off the cuts by the stretch of my hand, fetching and tidying the necessary tools. On my eighth birthday I was told that I would no longer be required to help my mother with tasks around the house but would work with my father for a few hours every day. So I learned as we worked together and my father poured into me the skills and know-ledge it had taken him a lifetime to acquire. Years later, when the palsy had begun to twist his hands and his breath was coming in shorter and shorter gasps, I was able to take the load from him. Silently, without a word spoken, the apprentice became the master. Before I knew it, it was he who was watching me work. And then he was gone.

And even when my career changed and I left the workshop behind forever, I still worked from the lessons I had learned at my father's side. People are not unlike trees: they too have unique and subtle markings. You have to read them, to know when your work is done. My father would never know what a task it was he had prepared me for. And for the rest of my life, whenever I experienced the press of wood against my skin, I thought of him and remembered the patience with which he had loved and taught me.

Why work?

How did Jesus get on with his dad? Not the Heavenly one – Scripture gives us all kinds of insight into that relationship. But what about the other one: his earthly dad Joseph, the carpenter who was human enough to consider divorcing his wife-to-be when he thought she had betrayed him and compassionate enough to step back from doing so when a dream let him know what was really going on?

Joseph was clearly there for the baby Jesus and there for the toddler who was taken into hiding in Egypt. Later on, the gospels talk about Jesus' mother and brothers, but Joseph gets no mention. Tradition has it that he died at some stage during Jesus' early life. We don't know when this was. Could the death of Joseph have been the traumatic event that pushed the thirty-year old Jesus to explore his own identity and destiny and ultimately begin his ministry? Or was it precisely the opposite – it was the absence of Joseph that held Jesus back *until* he was thirty, keeping him in the family business as provider to his mother and brothers?

Scripture is silent on these questions: but it does seem likely that Jesus knew his father for a good number of years before he died and that it was from Joseph that he learned his trade. Jesus later described his relationship with his Heavenly Father in the language of apprenticeship – 'the Son can do nothing by himself. He does only what he sees the Father doing.' Might he have been describing here a process he first learned in the carpentry workshop, at his human father's side? Might the learning principles that Jesus brought to *ministry* be the same principles he had learned in the world of work?

If so, then we should perhaps expect to see prayer and spirituality more as a process of craftsmanship than religious observance. In order to be free to leave his mother's home at thirty, had Jesus needed to pass on his own skills to a younger brother or cousin? Had he discovered in the workplace not only how to learn from a master, but how to teach an apprentice? The language of Jesus' discourse with his disciples and the model of learning he offers seem to bear this out and he invites us not only to walk with him – to grow in relationship and trust – but to work with him as well. On the foundation of relationship he builds a programme of active learning, asking us to invest in our own growth and development. We are invited to be intentional about our spiritual growth, to accept Jesus' challenge of work that will bring its own reward. If Jesus learned about learning in his time at the carpenter's bench, then he has lived inside the experience of growing in a craft, of gaining the skills and knowledge to do better with each new task, of honing those skills to their highest level of perfection, of patiently working away at this craft in the confidence that, with time, competence would come. And he has known, too, the joy of watching this process in another: of slowly, patiently teaching, of bringing the apprentice through the experiences and challenges from which learning will come. Jesus understands apprenticeship from both sides. This is a working

relationship, a journey into craftsmanship and competence. Jesus invites us to embrace the patience and hard
work that such a learning journey will require.

RESTLESS

Hungry for Heaven

The land is bleak with snow, clouds lour in the sky, there is a gale raging and the sea is a fury of waves, we are dying of hunger and there is no chance of human aid. Then let us storm Heaven with our prayers, asking that the same Lord who parted the Red Sea and fed His people in the desert take pity on us in our peril.
Early Celtic prayer recorded by Bede in The life of Cuthbert[25]

Worship does not satisfy our hunger for God – it whets our appetite.
Eugene Peterson[26]

The centre of Amsterdam is built on a concentric series of horse-shoe shaped canals, each bordered by the tall and often splendid houses that were once the homes of the merchants from whose wealth the city grew. With bicycles, cars, pedestrians and trams all competing to use the narrow tree-lined streets that run alongside and across these canals, Amsterdam today is a bustling, thriving, colourful metropolis: officially the world's most international city. During the middle years of the twentieth century it was also home to a large Jewish population: a population swelled by those who came west from Germany, fleeing the persecution of the increasingly violent Nazi party. When the Netherlands in turn fell to German occupation, life for the nation's Jewish population became more and more difficult. Thousands were deported to concentration camps while others went into hiding, often sheltered at great risk by their Dutch colleagues and neighbours.

Among these were the family of Anne Frank, who were hidden from July 1942 to August 1944 in a secret annexe (in Dutch the *Achterhuis*) of a house on the Prinsengracht. Just thirteen years old when she went into hiding, Anne Frank took with her a small book designed as an autograph book but pressed into service as a diary. Discovered by her father after the war and her death, Anne's diary was later published and has become one of the world's best-loved books. Her former hiding place is now a museum and one of Amsterdam's most popular tourist attractions. Writing in *Time* magazine's 1999 special edition *Time 100: The Most Important People of the Century*, Roger Rosenblatt says of Anne, 'The reason for her immortality was basically literary. She was an extraordinarily good writer, for any age and the quality of her work seemed a direct result of a ruthlessly honest disposition . . . Anne's deep effect on readers comes from her being a normal, if gifted, teenager. She was curious about sex, doubtful about religion, caustic about her parents, irritable especially to herself . . .'[27]

Anne's journal captures in intimate detail the daily routines of her grounded family and of the Dutch workers – employees of her father's firm – who put their own lives on the line to tend to their needs. But it also portrays with great eloquence the feelings of its author, the deeply human questions of a young girl. 'The passions the book ignites', Rosenblatt writes, 'suggest that everyone owns Anne Frank, that she has risen above the

Holocaust, Judaism, girlhood and even goodness and become a totemic figure of the modern world – the moral individual mind beset by the machinery of destruction, insisting on the right to live and question and hope for the future of human beings.'[28]

The poignancy with which she writes is magnified for us by our knowledge of her situation. She was, in so many ways, trapped: not only by the heavy bookcase that had been moved in front of the annexe door to keep her family hidden, but by the history that was unfolding around her, drawing millions into unimaginable horror. Because we know that Anne did not survive the war (her story would end in agony in Bergen-Belsen), we are all the more moved by her words. Typical of Anne's gift of self-reflection is this passage, dated February 12th, 1944

> Today the sun is shining, the sky is a deep blue, there is a lovely breeze and I am longing – so longing – for everything: to talk, for freedom, for friends, to be alone. And I do so long . . . to cry! I feel as if I am going to burst and I know that it would get better with crying; but I can't, I'm restless, I go from room to room, breathe through the crack of a closed window, feel my heart beating as if it is saying, 'can't you satisfy my longing at last?' I believe that it is spring within me; I feel that spring is awakening; I feel it in my whole body and soul. It is an effort to behave normally, I feel utterly confused. I don't know what to read, what to write, what to do, I only know that I am longing.[29]

Catholic scholar Ronald Rolheiser cites this passage in a meditation called *Longing is our spiritual lot*. He describes our deep human longings as a 'holy restlessness put in us by God to push us toward the infinite'.[30] 'There is in all of us', he writes, 'at the very centre of our lives, a tension, an aching, a burning in the heart that is insatiable, non-quietable and very deep.'[31] We picture Anne pacing through the rooms she cannot leave; sensing the coming of spring to the outside air, but unable to run out and taste it; trying to understand and master the conflicting emotions rising in her and we know that these are human longings. We share her restlessness and we know that somehow, in the mystery of our different lives, that this is what it *means* to be human. 'It is non-negotiable', Rolheiser concludes. 'If you are alive, you are restless, full of spirit. What you do with that spirit is your spiritual life.'[32]

Hungry hearts

In common with writers on prayer over many centuries, Rolheiser has discovered that there is a vital relationship between spirituality and hunger. To be restless, to be dissatisfied is part of our calling in the life of prayer: even though we spend so much of our time and resources – and indeed of our prayers – in seeking satisfaction. 'Blessed are those who hunger and thirst for righteousness' (Mt. 5:6, NIV), Jesus said. In a world in which we will do everything we can to escape hunger, how can it be described as a blessing? Why would we welcome this feeling of need? Why would the God who offers Sabbath rest want us to be restless? Because God has called us not only to walk with him but to work with him, embracing the intentionality of a relationship in which we are willing to invest. We know instinctively that a deep truth is hidden here. The words of Augustine that 'our hearts are restless until they find their rest in you' ring true in our experience.

Though we may speak of the *rest* that prayer brings to us, we also want to speak of the *restlessness* that gives prayer meaning. In the interaction between our human condition and our desire to know God, there is an intimate connection between *longing* and prayer. Though we find ourselves searching in so many ways for ease and comfort, something in us cries that ease and comfort will not save us. In the deepest part of ourselves, we know that godly dissatisfaction has a role to play in our growth – there is a hunger inherent in the life of prayer without which it has no power. In *Reaching for the Invisible God* Philip Yancey makes the same strong connection, citing the words of Meister Eckhart: 'The soul must long for God in order to be set aflame by God's love, but if the soul cannot yet feel this longing, then it must long for the longing. To long for the longing is also from God.'[33]

Though founded on the ancient traditions of the church, this suggestion that restlessness and longing are important in the life of prayer – that hunger has a role to play in teaching us – may prove particularly significant in the contemporary West, where our stomachs are full and the meeting of needs is the very basis of our culture. The fuller we are, the harder it is to embrace hunger. The more convenient it is to reach for comfort, the more difficult it is to reach for depth. Having built a global economy on the urge for gratification, it is counter-cultural to build faith on the urge for restraint: but if hunger is indeed a part of our journey, it is a battle we must face. If it is true that there are landscapes to be explored in the with-God life that can only be reached through hunger, then it is essential that we learn what hunger means. Scripture, history and the experience of Christians across the world all tell us that there is learning to be done in this area. As we walk with Christ, growing in and building on the relationship that has become central to our lives, our journey into deeper fields of prayer will touch on issues of restlessness and hunger in three key areas:

- **As an aspect of our learning and growth**. We struggle to embrace the restlessness of prayer because hunger and thirst are not comfortable feelings – they are conditions we instinctively seek to avoid. How are we to understand the complementary roles of rest and restlessness in our life with God: the one impulse calling us to satisfaction, the other calling us to need? What is the rightful place of hunger in our lives as we move towards maturity in Christ? Can the restlessness of our souls be harnessed to motivate us for the work that prayer demands?

- **In the interface of faith and culture**. To truly engage with hunger in the way the Bible asks us to will mean taking a stand against the very nature of the culture in which we live. Consumer culture teaches us to seek the satisfaction of our needs. If Scripture is teaching us to listen to our needs and to let their *dissatisfaction* drive us more deeply into God, the two cultures will clash. How can our life of prayer help us to anticipate and manage this confrontation well?

- **In exploring the specific discipline of fasting**. The relationship of hunger to prayer is nowhere made clearer than in the biblical concept of fasting. By linking prayer directly with the most basic form of consumption known to us – food – fasting allows the physical experience of hunger to represent and thereby illuminate our spiritual state. Fasting allows us not only to explore the meaning of hunger in our lives but also to discover just how shackled we are to our need for comfort. It challenges us to divert some of the energy we commit to consumption into an equally energized search for God.

Breakfast in Babylon

All three of these important threads come together in the true story of a hunger-strike undertaken by four young political prisoners in the ancient world – one of the stories that had a significant impact on the life of Jesus.[34] It is a story in which there is much to learn about hunger and prayer and in which faith triumphs in a hostile setting through the discipline of fasting. Recorded for us in Daniel (Dan. 1) the story tells of four young men taken by force from their homes and placed under house arrest in the city of Babylon: a city whose language, culture, religion and society are new to them.

The four are part of a larger group taken into exile by the Emperor Nebuchadnezzar. The aim is *assimilation*: Daniel and his friends are amongst the best educated young people of Jerusalem and the plan is that they should be re-educated in the culture and ways of Babylon. They will learn new languages and the names of new gods and be taught to see the world from the perspective of their conquerors. After a period of intense learning they will emerge as committed citizens of Babylon, acknowledging the superiority of Nebuchadnezzar's world over their primitive Hebrew culture. This at least is the theory and in return for cooperating with this reorientation, the exiles will be housed and fed and ultimately offered employment.

Daniel emerges very quickly as a leader and takes upon himself the responsibility of subverting the re-education programme. He needs to find some way that his team can not only survive Babylon but thrive there, and do so without losing their Hebrew faith and identity. How do you hold onto your roots when you have already been physically uprooted and are now to be subjected to the intentional uprooting of your intellectual, emotional and religious identity? How do you hold to the integrity of your inner world while your outer world is changing so fast and your fate is beyond your personal control?

We are not told in the text exactly why Daniel chose food as his battlefield. His choice perhaps reflects the Jewish idea that food is central to the spiritual life, but his chosen menu is not derived entirely from adherence to Jewish food laws. There is also the idea that by taking the king's food Daniel would be accepting his patronage: resisting the tasty and tempting food would symbolize a degree of independence. Beyond both of these, though, it is likely that Daniel was looking for something, *anything*, that would enable him to exercise the inner discipline of faith. He takes the initiative to organize a partial food fast and to gain the support of his guardians in doing so: while others on the programme benefit from the rich foods brought to them from the king's table, Daniel and his friends will live on vegetables and water. The result is a major triumph and Daniel's group emerges as the best of the best, despite the limitations of their diet.

The fast is not a public protest – no-one is to know that it is even happening – but as a private decision it speaks of strength and focus. And it will prove that God is with the Hebrew exiles. How else could they do so well on this limited diet, while their competitors had all the rich foods they could ask for? Daniel wants his fellow Hebrews to know that their God is able to sustain them, even in this bleak new place. He uses the discipline of a partial food fast as a tool for training in faith: for his own benefit and that of his companions. He takes the Babylonian School of

Culture and turns it into a Hebrew School of Faith and it won't be long before his friends find out – in a blast furnace heated to seven times its normal operating temperature – just how effective the training has been.

As an aspect of learning and growth, this experience is vital to the young Hebrew exiles. It comes at a stage in their lives when they are still forming their adult habits and attitudes and urgently asking how they will respond to their ongoing exile. Discoveries made and habits formed at this stage can last well into later years, which is exactly what we see with Daniel. In his later experiences we see the fruits of the understanding of prayer forged in these early trials. In his finest moment, the world-famous confrontation years later with the new king Darius and his lions (Dan. 6), Daniel's faith is built on an unbreakable daily routine of prayer. Ernest Lucas says that

> The stories of Daniel make clear that one reason for this (his extraordinary spirit) was his intimacy with God, expressed and maintained by prayer. It was his regular habit of prayer that gave him the strength to ignore the king's new law. To have changed that habit, giving the appearance of fearing the king more than God, would have affected his intimacy with God, whom he would have felt he had betrayed in some measure.[35]

Daniel's later determination not to break the pattern of prayer, even once, is a statement not only of his faith and determination but of his own self-awareness. He has come to realize that his need of God is greater than any other need – even the need for the favour of the king. Daniel is immune to bullying and bribery simply because his need to pray is greater. He knows which hunger matters more. The same strength of faith is proved in the lives of Shadrach, Meshach and Abednego as they face their own life or death struggle at the furnace (Dan. 3). Their confidence is in the character of goodness of God – he can be trusted even if the king turns against them. What can we learn from this in our own cultural exile?

- That part of our growth in prayer comes in learning to 'harness hunger' – to let the deepest longings of our hearts, our inner restlessness and passion, flow *into* rather than *against* our life with God.
- That the *discipline of going without* – whether food or some other comfort – has a part to play in teaching us to pray.
- That a chosen, focused, intentional approach to prayer can give us clarity in the face of cultural assimilation, building our capacity, in all the right ways, to resist.

In the interface of faith and culture, this story has rich resources to offer us. Walter Brueggemann has written extensively on the theology of exile.

> The text invites people like us, at the door of capitulation, to think about an alternative. The proffered alternative is this: Remember *who* you are by remembering *whose* you are. Be your own person even in the face of the empire, of the dominant ideology, of the great power of death . . . Be your own person, because God has not succumbed to the weight of the empire.[36]

Daniel's chosen food-fast has a lot to do with this remembering. Cultural change, for Daniel, should not be allowed without question to lead to a changed identity, no matter how powerful or all-embracing the culture is.

You are who you are because God is who God is and even if the culture around you has forgotten this, burying the voice of God in the chaos of a thousand other voices, there are ways in which you can resist – and remember. Ajith Fernando sees this as the triumph of Daniel's life: 'Daniel and his friends were fully immersed in a pagan culture. They worked hard and succeeded in society. But they did not compromise their religious principles. They challenge the position of those who say it is impossible to be totally committed to God and his principles in a fallen world.'[37]

How does this speak to our journey in prayer?

- It tells that there is a connection between *prayer* and *identity*. Will your identity be shaped without question by the cultural forces surrounding you, or will your longing for another story – God's story – be strong enough to shape you differently?
- It tells us that there is a connection between *prayer* and *memory*. The unmet longing at the heart of human experience comes about in part because we have forgotten who we are. We have lost our first home, our first friendship and our first language and all three call to us. To turn to prayer is to listen to this longing and to open our hearts to the journey homewards. If you don't know who you are, how can you know your way home? Remembering is the beginning of return.
- Lastly, it tells us of the connection between *prayer* and *struggle*. Daniel goes without easy food because he knows that an easy life is a life built on a lie. He is not afraid to take on the struggle of a limited diet because he understands that hearing God's voice amid the noise will be, by definition, a

struggle. An exilic life is lived in the face of competing narratives: different voices clamouring for
our attention. Daniel is intentional about giving his
attention to Yahweh and he knows that this will be
a battle.

In exploring the specific discipline of fasting, this story
teaches us the power of going without. Daniel sees and
embraces the connection between spiritual longing and
physical hunger. By attaching prayer to the discipline of
fasting he points to several lessons that, centuries later,
still have meaning for us:

- He gives the inner reality of his hunger for God an
  outward expression in fasting. In this way his body
  becomes the trigger for the passions of his soul. Every
  time he feels hungry, his spirit is reminded why.
- He places prayer, by definition, in the very centre of
  everyday life. There is no human need more basic
  than hunger and no human activity more rhythmic
  and regular than eating. By urging his friends to
  join him in this fast, Daniel gives them the opportunity to remember their God and their goals every
  time a guard comes towards them with a tray. It is
  perhaps intriguing to explore how much this decision – to bring prayer to mind with every meal –
  impacted Daniel's life-long habit of praying three
  times each day (Dan. 6:10). By letting his hunger for
  food stimulate his hunger for God, Daniel establishes prayer at the very centre of his life. To put the
  same observation in the form of a question: if you
  thought of God as often as you think of food, how
  might your prayer life change?
- He regains inner *control* even though his outer life
  is controlled by others. The exiles have been placed

in a situation in which they have little opportunity to exercise choice: their freedoms have been taken from them. But by finding one area in which choice is possible, Daniel is able to offer that choice to God as an act of worship. The empire has placed him in a virtual prison cell, but by choosing an even smaller cell, his prison becomes an act of surrender to God that he has freely chosen. The empire can stop him from escaping outwards from exile, but it cannot stop him from claiming inner freedom. Prisoners of conscience over the centuries have likewise discovered that an incarceration voluntarily surrendered to God as an act of worship does gain a certain inner freedom and reduces the oppressor's power. In the inner landscape of prayer, freedom is always a choice.

Life in the fast lane

These same lessons have shaped and informed those seeking a God-ward life over centuries. Fasting is a discipline often lost to the church, but it is a discipline whose rediscovery seems always to accompany renewal. The connections Daniel and his friends discovered between the inward hunger of the soul and the outward hunger of the body have borne rich fruit in every generation of the church, bringing many into the deeper places of prayer where the longings of the heart ignite the life of the spirit.

Central to this experience is the sense that we are always in some way exiles. This planet is our home in the deepest possible sense: not only given to us but *made for us*. earth is created for us and we are created for earth. But the empires we have constructed on this planet – the assumptions we make, the cities we build and the cultures we construct – are always in some measure alien to our true nature as children of God. We have built foreign kingdoms on top of the true land God has given us and our restlessness is a measure of our homelessness.

As we grow in prayer, walking with Jesus and learning the rhythms of his ways, we will find that the very act of prayer awakens in us the longing for our true home and that this, in turn, can fuel our prayer. Jesus reminds us who we are and who our Father is. As this memory floods us and we realize how out of line with it our lives have become, a new hunger grips us: a hunger captured in the words 'Let *your* empire come, let *your* will be done on our earth as it is in your Heaven.' Our inward longing for God becomes an outward longing to see God's purposes fulfilled. We begin to dream of Babylon redeemed by the power and presence of the same God who has won and warmed our own inner worlds. But we will not see this dream fulfilled without passion: without a longing so deep that it gnaws our spirits as surely as an empty stomach lets us know of its need. If we are not seeing enough of God's redemptive beauty breaking into our lives, is it because we are not hungry enough? Leonard Ravenhill wrote in a previous generation

> The church has many organisers, but few agonisers; many who pay, but few who pray; many resters, but few wrestlers; many who are enterprising, but few who are interceding. The secret of praying is praying in secret. That is the difference between the modern church and the Early Church. In the matter of effective praying, never have so many left so much to so few. Let us pray![38]

The opening words of Ephesians 6:12 in the King James Version – 'for we wrestle not' – are all too often true of our lives and all too often as far as we read.

How can we embrace in our own time and culture a faith informed by the passion and focus of Daniel and his friends? Here are some places we might start:

- **Build your life of prayer on a longing for God**. Run after his presence. Seek focus, clarity, passion. Tell God you want this relationship; or if you can't get that far, that you want to want it; or if that is too difficult, that you want to want to want it; or if even that is too high a price, that you want to want to want to want it. Whatever your starting point, take a step towards a life of prayer driven by desire to know God.

- **Learn to harness hunger**. Experiment with fasting – perhaps gently at first, since you may well discover it to be a much harder fight than you have expected. Explore different modes of fasting, from short-term periods of complete hunger to longer-term adoption of partial and specific abstinences. Try living without a single drop of alcohol for three months. Fast from television for a week. Choose to live without your laptop, phone or iPod for a few days or even a few minutes. Don't give things up as a simple test of strength; do it as a means of redirecting your time, attention and energy to the one who walks beside you.

- **Linger longer in your longings**. As you pray, let the passions God stirs in your heart shape your experience. Live *inside* your longing for home, your restlessness for change. In extended periods of prayer, such as in a 24/7 room, be willing to expose your deepest dreams to the light of God's presence.

Ask God to clarify and sanctify your longings, until your heart begins to beat with his heart. Let that which breaks the heart of God break into yours. Pray that your imagination will be ignited by God's purposes, then pray for that which you imagine. 'If God can do more than we can ask or imagine', Dave Davidson has written, 'why not ask for more imagination?'[39]

- **Make the choice**. Without doubt the key to Daniel's story is that he *chose* to put God first. In the face of the empire's threats and promises he chose to turn his heart to God. This choice – to make time for God; to create space in our hearts and lives for his presence; to actively pursue relationship; to long for what he longs for; to seek daily opportunities to be with him; to believe that prayer matters – is essential to growth in prayer. This is a choice I must make if I am to grow and it is a choice no-one else can make for me. The one lie about prayer that we most fall prey to and most need to be rid of is that we can grow in prayer by accident. Prayer is volitionally conditioned: its impact on us is closely linked to our desire. There is no technique in prayer, no approach or formula, no spiritual exercise that will do you any good at all unless you want them to.

- **Know what you're missing**. In the life of prayer, as in so many challenges that face us, there is no choosing for x without choosing against y. The decision to move in a particular direction is often a decision, just as intentionally, not to move in another. In fasting, the choice to embrace discomfort for the sake of growth is equally a choice not to seek comfort. There will be a cost to pursuing God in this way and some of the choices that might otherwise be open to you – to enjoy the many benefits of a consumerist, needs-based culture – might unexpectedly become closed. Learn what it means to make your choice, to remember and to hold to it when alternative offers are made.

Become passionate about prayer. Be willing to make the investment. Set your heart on transformation. Hungry prayer is prayer that acknowledges the longing for God and finds God in every longing. As Daniel and his friends found and as thousands like them have discovered in the centuries since, as Jesus himself promised, you will not be short-changed. The pathway of prayer, driven by our passion for God's purposes, is the pathway to life. 'So, hold unshakeably to the heart of our faith, which is Jesus Christ our hope – born, crucified and risen, during the time when Pontius Pilate was governor. Let nothing turn you aside from that hope.'[40]

Prayer: Promised and Assured

You call
To my broken heart,
You see my craving for companionship,
My desperation for depth
And dependency.
You notice
My need to be known,
Yet know I am afraid
To be familiar
You feel that I fear your freedom
Yet you hear my heart:

And hungry for the healing
That is promised and assured,
I come to you.

You accept my condition,
You receive my resolution;
My deep determination,
To press on, to wrestle
Pursuing restoration.
Let all that is in me be open
To your operation:
Not closed to your correction,
Not averse to your intervention.
As you reshape my soul:

And hungry for the hope
That is promised and assured,
I come to you.

You restore my image,
You shine my scratched surface.

You find diamonds
Where there has been dullness,
And bring gloss
Where there has been gloom:
Pouring peace into the places
Perverted by past pains
You repaint my planet

And hungry for the Heaven
That is promised and assured,
I come to you.

Gerard and Chrissie Kelly

Exercises

With or without . . .

Part One: Take a specific food or luxury that you really enjoy, such as chocolate, and let it represent a specific area in your life in which you see a need for change and growth, for example patience. Fast from the food for a specific time and use the opportunity to pray into that area of your life. Every time you think of the luxury you so miss, take a moment to ask God to change you in the area you have been struggling with. Ask that that he would minister to your struggle and work deeply at the root of this need, dealing with whatever it is that causes you to be so vulnerable in this area.

Part Two: When the period of fasting is over, celebrate in faith all God has done and is doing by eating that food again with thanksgiving and joy. But from now on, each time you enjoy it, keep the association with prayer going, by thanking God for working in you in that area and asking for his grace and strength to grow! So if you have chosen chocolate and patience, you will let the absence of chocolate in your life remind you to pray and then, because of the association you have made, you will let the presence of chocolate in your life remind you again.

Harness the hard times

Often we run from times of discomfort and struggle because we see these times as getting in the way of our joy. For Daniel, the time of struggle was exactly the time to take action and seek God. In truth, it is during the times of struggle that we find the deepest wells of faith and strength, wells we just don't access in the more comfortable phases of our lives. It is often in our most *restless* times that God is most revealed to us. During these times there are very specific things we can do:

- Make conscious choices to search through prayer and in Scripture for revelation and encouragement
- Ask others to pray for us that we will lean into God and not away from him
- Punctuate each day, start and end, with an invitation to God to hold us through our trials Make an appropriate use of the discipline of fasting to bring focus and to wrestle with the possible outcome of the trial
- Stimulate our senses throughout the day and night with that which will keep us facing toward God – reading or listening to words that encourage, using music
- Take time to seek out the places of peace that have most helped us in the past to find the presence of God
- Take a specific Scripture, word or song and recite it when feeling overwhelmed – make it a prayer for sustenance and strength
- Ask God to use the hunger that this trial brings – our restlessness, our longing for change – as a positive force in our growth and in his purposes
- Pray that *in this* his kingdom will come and his will be done: just as Jesus found strength in the words 'I want your will, not mine' (Lk. 22:42).

Develop your dreams

Make it a regular part of your prayer life to talk to God about the things you long for. Make it one of the goals of your prayers to ask God to refine your dreams, so you come close to longing for the things he longs for. Ask him for a passion that you can *trust* as the foundation of your prayers. Learn to allocate time in your life of prayer to developing, refining and expressing this passion. Use journalling, drawing and creative imagining to try to identify the things that drive you – the changes you most long to see in the world – and bring these before God. Using Scripture, prayer, study and the advice of others you trust, try to hold these dreams up against the revealed will of God. Let God's refining presence shape your dreams into sails, then pray without reserve for the wind of his Spirit to come . . .

Sit right down and write yourself a letter

If you are living through a period in which the process described above is very real to you – you are very aware of your own dreams and are hearing God speak into them – write a letter to the 'you' of three, six or twelve months ahead. Tell yourself what you are hoping for, what you care about. Seal it, date it and put it away. When the time comes to open it, get ready to pray: with joy and thanksgiving for the things God has done, with renewed passion and energy for the things that have yet to be, and with sober longing for the dreams that have died.

Blessing

When you are too full to care
Too frightened to dare
Too free to be aware
When your needs are so well met
You haven't truly felt them yet

May God give you
The gift of hunger
And in your hunger
May he fill you

When distractions catch you
And the markets throw their magic at you
When hawking voices
Hijack choices
And you chase the toys
You're told you'll need
Replacing deeper joys
That love might feed
When you taste the treats that tempt
But leave you empty

May God give you
The gift of hunger
And in your hunger
May he fill you

If your heart is hollow
For want of a dream
If your soul is shallow
Your spirit, lean
If you face

Emaciation
For lack of true
Imagination

May God give you
The gift of hunger
And in your hunger
May he fill you

Gerard Kelly

RICH

Called to Creativity

When God purposes to work He first sets His people to
pray.

John Wesley

The very narrative of faith which we seek to know
and to live is symbolically expressed in our space. We
take the ordinary aspects of life – stone, wood, windows, tables and chairs – and form them into voices of
the Christian mystery. Space becomes the visual
image of the connection between the known and the
unknown.

Robert Webber[41]

Several years ago we were helping to lead a worship
celebration at Spring Harvest in the UK. There were
thousands of people present in the huge tent but right
at the front, close to the platform, was a group we held
in particular esteem. They had come as a group and
were held together by a common experience: they
were adults with learning disabilities. One among
them had Down's Syndrome and had become known
to us during the week by the sheer exuberance of her
presence and praise. She would sing, dance, draw,

paint: whatever media were made available with which to express worship, she would engage with passion and abandon.

On one particular evening we were exploring the meaning of the death of Christ. A wooden cross had been placed at the front of the platform, as a helpful if predictable visual aid. We had worshipped together, meditated on the events surrounding Christ's crucifixion and were now considering from Scripture just what we might do to grasp the meanings of this ancient event. We wan-ted to communicate the historic, flesh-and-blood reality of the death of Christ: the event described in the ancient Kralice Bible of the Czech Brethren as Jesus' 'terrible offering of blood'. We encouraged those present to embrace the harsh reality of this event, to sense in their imagination what it might be to experience the very real and present substance of the cross, to run their fingers over the roughness of its wood. Partway through this exercise of the imagination, we looked across to Natalie. She had risen from her seat, come forward to the very edge of the platform, reached upwards and grasped the base of our wooden cross with both hands. Her eyes closed, her face tight with the agony of imagining, she was running her hands across the wood: feeling, with every fibre of her being, the reality of the cross. Never have we seen a more beautiful response to the invitation to imagine and never a more perfect picture of the meaning of *sacrament*: holy truth accessible in sensory experience.

Natalie's lack of inhibition in taking literally the invitation to 'feel the reality of the cross' is illustrative precisely because it is such an exception. Most of us are too inhibited or too reserved or, in our own estimation, too sophisticated for such an act. Our faith resides for the most part in the realm of cerebral assent: it is virtual, invisible, grounded in a series of mental affirmations. Our life of prayer and worship for the most part matches this condition: it draws on words, thoughts, silences and sometimes music, but rarely strays more deeply into the sensory realm. We *think* our prayers – we don't often see, touch, taste or feel them. Even where tradition has bequeathed us a handful of sensory experiences: the smell of incense, the glow of a stained glass window, the silent presence of a statue or icon, many of us have run away from precisely these gifts. Desperate to lift the stifling blankets of empty tradition from our worship, some of us have flushed several babies away in the dirty bathwater we so despise.

What can we do to come to our senses in prayer? What place does the hard work of creativity, artfulness and self-expression have in our life with God? The importance of these questions for our time is perhaps shown by the extent to which the richness of art – an embracing of creative gifts at the heart of worship and prayer – is an important factor in many of the ways in which young people are reshaping their experience of faith, from the chaotic beauty of 24/7 prayer rooms to the refined installations and events of the alternative worship movement and the emerging church.

God's mobile home

The richness of worship and prayer is one of the deepest traditions of the Christian and Jewish faiths and has its origin at the very start of it all, in the creation of the *tabernacle*, the mobile prayer-centre that travelled with the Hebrew people through their wilderness years. God's instructions to Moses establish for all time the *priority* of prayer and worship in the community of faith and set in place some of the principles by which the *nature* of prayer and worship will be defined. Among these is the significant role of art and creativity as the life-blood of the pursuit of faith. The tabernacle is not a thrown together jumble sale of spirituality. It is finely crafted, beautifully conceived and made: a canvas cathedral worthy of the God in whose name it stands. Part Tate-Modern, part 24/7 prayer room, part Westminster Abbey, the tabernacle is a place of beauty and stillness, of peace and prayer, of spiritual encounter and aesthetic celebration. This is a *rich* experience of prayer: resourceful, intentional, creative and heartfelt. Unlike many of our experiences of prayer, the one thing it isn't is dull.

Scholars tell us that 'Nearly one-third of the book of Exodus is devoted to considerations regarding the tabernacle, Israel's wilderness sanctuary.'[42] Chapters 25 to 31 are taken up with the detailed instructions for the completion of this movable feast of worship, a mobile home for God in the midst of his people. Clearly there is intentionality here about placing worship and prayer at the heart of the community. The structure of the book of Exodus reflects the understanding that has shaped the Jewish faith and still does: and that gave birth in turn to the Christian understanding that in the midst of secular life there should be a place for worship. Just as Sabbath talks about a rhythm of sacred *time* woven through our lives, so the tabernacle speaks of sacred *space*. The holiness of this one space does not render the other places we live in less sacred. Rather it establishes the basis on which all of life is sacred – because God dwells in the midst of us. The defining characteristic of the people of Israel was that God was with them. Their strength, identity and purpose all came from this one fact and the tabernacle was the vehicle by which the Lord would make his presence known.

> 'The sanctuary is not simply a symbol of the divine presence; it is *an actual vehicle for divine immanence.*'[43]

The tabernacle takes the *idea* that 'God is with us' and gives it roots and reality. It asks 'How can we celebrate this idea? How can we be reminded that God is with us? How can we let the fact that God is with us shape our lives? How can we live all our lives in the light of God's presence with us?'

Threads of learning

The detailed design of the tabernacle is such that Christians through the ages have drawn endless parallels and analogies, but the principle value of this account is in what it tells us about the place of prayer and worship at the centre of our lives and about the intentionality (aka work) with which we might approach this aspect of our calling. Jesus calls us not only to walk with him but to work with him, to invest in the life of prayer – to cooperate in the creation of a tabernacle that will be the vehicle of God's presence with us. In my private life of prayer, in my individual efforts to know and embrace God's presence, why should I not expend the same effort and intention the Hebrews were asked to expend? Is prayer a duty to be performed or a craft to be learned? Is it utility or art? Am I reciting a shopping list or dancing a dance? Are there talents I can use in prayer and skills I can learn, as a carpenter might learn to use his father's tools?

What are the marks of the tabernacle story from which we can learn in our own growth in prayer?

Firstly, that the call is to invest every aesthetic gift we have been given in this process: this sacred space is a *resourceful* space.

The key people called by God to work with Moses on the creation of worship are not pastors or organizers but artists. They are filled with the Spirit of God and with 'wisdom, intelligence and skill in all kinds of crafts' (Ex. 35:30). As Creator, God is the Author of their gifting. As Spirit he is the one who anoints their work. These are the first people in all history described as being filled with the Spirit of God– and they are artists. Is it wrong to infer from this passage that spirituality is by definition creative and that the life of prayer, properly understood, will be a life lived artfully? Rich prayer is prayer that acknowledges the creativity of God the Creator and the artfulness of his human creatures, made in his image, and seeks to express relationship in the meeting of the two.

To connect with the Creator is to connect with creativity. God is life and beauty, art and artfulness. For many of us it is in art and music that we catch our first glimpses of him. And so it should be. All beauty points to the source of beauty: artfulness itself is the dusting of the fingerprints of God. All artists are prophets, whether they acknowledge it or not, because they point, by their very artfulness, to the remnant DNA of the creative God in all of us. The journey of prayer is a journey of beauty, of inspiration, of deep *joy* in the C.S. Lewis understanding of the word: moments of aesthetic experience so rich, so life-affirming that they cast technicolour shadows on the dirt floors of our ordinary world. To seek God is to seek glory. To touch God is to touch beauty. How could such a touch not awaken in us the most profound response of human joy?

This is the tradition by which the icon painters of the Eastern Orthodox churches are driven. In her studies of the churches of Russia, Jenny Robertson records an interview with a painter of icons: 'We paint the lives of saints, but we're concerned with something more than biography, we preach the Gospel, but we use no words. Our work uses created things, wood and linen, chalk, organic materials, egg yolk, lapis lazuli, gold, linseed oil, resins, amber. We offer them back to the Creator.'[44]

Secondly, that worship makes a claim for priority in our lives: we are called to the *intentional* work of creating sacred space.
The essence of the extensive biblical material of the tabernacle is beautifully captured in one short passage in Exodus 31

> The LORD also said to Moses, 'Look, I have chosen Bezalel son of Uri, grandson of Hur, of the tribe of Judah. I have filled him with the Spirit of God, giving him great wisdom, intelligence and skill in all kinds of crafts. He is able to create beautiful objects from gold, silver and bronze. He is skilled in cutting and setting gemstones and in carving wood. Yes, he is a master at every craft!' (Ex. 31:1–5).

This introduces the great adventure of creating the tabernacle. Bezalel is given an assistant, Oholiab (Ex. 31:6) and whole teams of other artists and craftsmen are recruited to work with them (Ex. 35:10). The people are given the opportunity to contribute gold and silver, fine linen and threads: all the beautiful and valuable resources with which the tabernacle will be made (Ex. 35:5–9). Significant artistic talents; finely-honed craftsmanship; quality materials; the gifts of many people – these are the ingredients of which worship is created in the wilderness. This is to be a place in which the best is given to God, a space of beauty and peace inspired by God's Spirit.

Significantly, in between the moment when God tells Moses to construct the tabernacle and the point at which he rallies the people to the task, they have been using these same gifts and materials to create a golden calf to worship. In Moses' absence, the people have panicked and have forged a false worship from these same God-given resources. Perhaps even Bezalel and Oholiab were caught up, with Joshua, in this terrible misuse of talent. Gifts that are not surrendered to God will be surrendered to idols: the act of bringing art into worship is an act not only of submission to God but of resistance to the dominant idols of the culture that would happily hijack those same talents.

The people contribute; the artists work; God gives the design – here is a picture of worship in which we co-operate with our Creator to make space for his presence in our lives. It is intentional, focused, deliberate work: an investment in a relationship that matters to us. What does it mean for you, thousands of years later, to work towards the making of a tabernacle?

> The tabernacle was very costly in time, effort and monetary value; yet in its significance and function it pointed to the chief end of man: to glorify God and to enjoy him forever. Above every other consideration was the fact that the omnipotent, unchanging, and transcendent God of all the universe had, by means of the tabernacle, graciously come to 'dwell' or 'tabernacle' with his people . . .[45]

Thirdly, that this exercise of creativity reflects the creativity of God: our *creative* response honours his creative action in our lives.

Recent scholarship has drawn attention to the central importance of the creation to the Exodus narrative. The God who liberates the Hebrew slaves is the Maker of Heaven and earth and as they come to know him and bring their lives into line with his purposes, they are restored to the order and beauty with which they were first created. Similarly, the work of the tabernacle re-establishes, in the chaos and dust of the wilderness, the benevolent rule of God. 'At this small, lonely place in the midst of the chaos of the wilderness', Terence Fretheim writes, 'a new creation comes into being. In the midst of disorder, there is order.'[46] Central to this order is the conviction that the creative gifting of the artists is a reflection of the creativity of God. Their work mirrors his.

> Bezalel executes in miniature the divine creative role of Genesis 1 in the building of the tabernacle. The spirit of God with which the craftsmen are filled is a sign of the living, breathing force that lies behind the completing of the project just as it lies behind the creation. Their intricate craftsmanship mirrors God's own work.[47]

There is a creative dimension to our lives of worship and prayer because there is a creative dimension to *who we are*, reflecting the creative dimension of *who God is*. To pursue prayer and worship without thought to creative expression is to rob God of the fuller picture of himself that worship intends: it is to show in monochrome a film made in technicolour, to represent as flat a design made to be three-dimensional. Our poverty of expression robs God of the colours of his glory and robs us of the many ways of knowing him he has provided for.

> Creativity is what God is all about, we're made in his image. Leaders, pre-occupied with the five m's – meetings,

music, ministry, miracles and money, have neglected movement, colour, taste, smell and touch. We must use all means to celebrate and communicate the love God has for people and the joys and pains we experience in our struggle to know him.[48]

Fourthly, that this model speaks both to our corporate lives of worship and to our individual lives of prayer: that which the tabernacle does for the community is mirrored in the *heartfelt* response we each make.

If the account of the creation of the tabernacle spoke only to our corporate worship lives, it would already have a great deal to say to us. But it goes further. It is a model that should shape not only our gathered worship and those responsible for planning worship events. It is for all of us and for the whole of our lives. John's gospel makes this clear by borrowing from the language of tabernacle to explore the incarnation of Jesus. When he describes Jesus as the one who 'became human and lived here on earth among us' (Jn. 1:14), scholars believe he is deliberately invoking the idea of tabernacle. Jesus 'tabernacles among us' and incarnation becomes the model by which we in turns are called to live.

The Spirit is given to each one of us so that the presence of Jesus goes where we go. The risen Christ is present in the world through his presence in the church and in each believer. The tabernacling of God becomes a question of each surrendered heart: so Paul is able to claim Christians are a 'temple of the Holy Spirit' (1 Cor. 3:16) and Peter calls us as living stones to be built into God's dwelling place (1 Pet. 2:5). Whatever craft and intentionality went into the making of the tabernacle and then the temple now goes into the shaping of our lives, alone and together. You are the meeting place of Heaven and earth, the arena of encounter with God, the sacred space wherein his presence dwells. This means that the order and beauty that come to the wilderness through the work of Bezalel and his colleagues come to your desert world every time you, too, worship.

Our worship and the surrender of our gifts to God's anointing become the means by which the desert places reconnect with their creational fruitfulness and rest. Every heart that bows the knee to Christ becomes a tabernacle in the world. The truly rich life is not a life of high expenditure but a life lived gracefully, each day spent in optimal openness to the presence and participation of God. Prayer is not for 'gathered' moments alone – it is also for the fabric of my everyday. And whether worship is expressed in the assembly of God's people or in the tabernacle of the heart, it is intended to be richly artful worship: colourful, imaginative devotion that draws the very best out of our lives.

Prayer gives you wings

What will this mean for our journey deeper into the life of prayer? That Christ calls us to work with him on the building of a tabernacle, that all our gifts are needed, that the finest of resources will be used, that the richness of art and artfulness have a place in the growth of a praying heart. Alison Morgan suggests in her guide to prayer that 'There are many forms of prayer, and many approaches to prayer. One of the simplest descriptions of prayer is given by the catechism of the Roman Catholic church: *Prayer is the raising of the mind and heart to God*. A more modern definition goes like this: *Prayer is turning our whole being to God, and staying there . . .'*[49] But what will our whole being involve? Not the thought life alone, but the senses: all our faculties engaged in this relationship. In developing the Prayerhouse ministry for Spring Harvest in the UK, we have worked on a definition of prayer as 'All I am responding to all God is – in the light of all he is doing in the world.' We use 'all I am' intentionally to include our creative gifts, because we have personally experienced such liberation and depth from bringing creative gifting into prayer. We call this style of prayer 'wholehearted prayer' because it calls for a heartfelt response from deep within each one of us, brining our every energy to bear as we reach out to God.

This is not only a corporate concern, though art has a huge part to play in corporate worship. It is also for small gatherings; for groups; for 24/7 prayer rooms and similar projects – and for the individual in their own rhythm of regular prayer. Poetry and painting; words and music; maps and candles and images and post-it notes; stones and water and towels and leaves and wood; nails and chicken wire and those tiny plastic coloured beads you can buy in Ikea: these and more have been part of our vocabulary of prayer in recent years. We have drawn prayers, chanted prayers, dredged up prayers from the deep history of the church. Cameras and photocopiers and printers have become instruments of intercession; blackboards an arena for praise; Walkmans and iPods have shaped private moments – CD players and video projectors resourced gathered joy. And time after time we have discovered the richness and depth of prayer in such forms, when written words have captured prayers our hearts dared not speak; when drawings and paintings have expressed longings too deep for words, when minutes committed to prayer have turned into hours and seemed like an instant. Our prayers have still contained a lot of *thoughts* and *words*. We are not rejecting of the usual ways of praying – we are adding to them. But there is something in the creativity – in the releasing of gifts long ago buried in us by our God, given to us for such a time as this – that has given wings to our prayers.

> Don't let your worship decline to the performance of mere duty. Don't let the childlike awe and wonder be choked out by unbiblical views of virtue. Don't let the scenery and poetry and music of your relationship with God shrivel up and die. You have capacities for joy which you can scarcely imagine. They were made for the enjoyment of God. He can awaken them no matter how long they have lain asleep. Pray for his quickening power. Open your eyes to his glory. It is all around you. 'The heavens declare the glory of God and the firmament proclaims his handiwork.'[50]

Poetry and pottery

When you introduce someone for the first time to a more creative way of praying, for example in a 24/7 prayer room, and you hear them say that 'This is all a bit strange' and that 'I'm not really creative' and 'I'm not sure I can pray for more than a few minutes' and 'How will I know what to do?', then you speak to them as they leave eight hours later and they tell you that it seemed like a minute and that they could happily stay another eight hours and that God has met with them and spoken to them and that they never knew prayer could be like that . . . then you know that Bezalel and Oholiab have something to teach us. What would happen if not only our public worship but our private lives of prayer were opened up once more to the full breadth of the Creator's gifts, to the 'full foaming God of the sea and the sacraments'?[51] How might it change us to pursue a richer life of prayer? Perhaps, in the words of John Noble, it will mean, 'The dancers, film-makers, potters, weavers, poets, architects, builders, jewellers, administrators, cooks, teachers, initiators, servants and many, many more bringing their skills to restore and beautify the living temple of our living God, in a fitting tribute to the one who bled and died to make this new technicoloured age of grace, creativity and everlasting joy a reality.'[52]

How can this become a reality in your life of prayer? Are you in a position to initiate a 24/7 prayer week or set up a Prayerhouse and, for yourself and others, dive into an experience of creative, artful prayer? Is there scope in your own private prayers for creative expression; a journal to write in; a drawing pad; a corner of your room where art and icons can inspire you; prayers that move your body? Could you use photo-collage instead of relying on your memory to represent the people and places you pray for? Can you walk through the places God has called you to pray about? Are there resources that others have prepared – music; slide shows; images; writings – that can inspire and help you?

The idea of prayer with a footprint in the physical world – prayer that engages the senses and allows itself to inhabit surrendered materials – is not a new idea. It is more the recovery of ancient practice. But it is a recovery vital to our age for a number of reasons.

Sacred space

It is important because there is such a hunger in our age for sacred space. 'There is, in fact, a tremendous hunger now in the West to rediscover holy places. Places where tragic accidents happen are quickly turned into shrines, with flowers, candles, toys, photographs of the child struck down in a car accident, of the victim of violent crime.'[53] In a fast-paced and largely secularized world, many people long for a sense of the holy. Can our more creative understanding of prayer and worship respond to this need?

Sign and myth

It is also important because our culture is recovering its passion for non-verbal communication. In his now classic work *Transforming mission*, David Bosch predicted just this change. 'Metaphor, symbol, ritual, sign and myth, long maligned by those interested only in 'exact' expressions of rationality, are today being rehabilitated', he wrote. 'They not only touch the mind and its conceptions, and evoke action with a purpose, but compel the heart.'[54]

Screenagers in love

Post-modern culture is more visually oriented than the preceding age of modernity. Brian and Kevin Draper write 'TVs, CPUs, VCRs and VDUs – not books – have become the weapons of the contemporary revolution. Control the visual media and you win the war, whether it's Serb versus Croat or Coke versus Pepsi.'[55] The application of this truth to our faith is not entirely new, but the wider context is. In pre-modern churches there has always been a willingness to connect visually with God. Andrew Walker notes that 'We can see the different ways in which cultures have responded to Jesus in their religious iconography. The ancient Syrian Church of South India, for example, presents Jesus as the guru complete with turban. Quite naturally, the Ethiopian Jesus is black, and the Russian Orthodox Christ is Russified and noticeably softer and more recognisably human than the stylised and stern Jesus of Byzantium.'[56] Are there challenges in our age to have access to Jesus in more visual ways, to allow 'screenagers' to bring to prayer their heightened visual literacy?

None of these factors dictate that we *must* be more creative in our praying. Changes in culture do not by definition demand changes in our spirituality. But they do allow us room to experiment – they invite us to discover new ways of prayer. And since the new is for the most part old, the invitation is not so much to reinvent prayer as to rediscover it: to explore in our own time and context what the call of God to Bezalel and Oholiab was all about and what believers across the centuries have known. And these conditions also tell us that our times are favourable to a more creative approach to prayer. We ourselves are children of these times – so we ourselves can benefit from colouring our prayer lives. Those around us, too, might find our lives less strange and our faith more accessible, if our prayers more often took shape as something they could touch and taste. What can you do to bring the richness and colour of Bezalel's tabernacle to your prayers?

Exercises

Lifting holy hands

This prayer exercise has been developed to be simple and memorable and to make use of a visual aid that for most of us is always available: the fingers of our hands. Try using it for a while, or be inspired by it to create your own small rituals, using your body to engage in prayer. It suggests a brief prayer for each finger, reflecting the special role of each:

- The thumb, which all the four fingers need, reminds us of our dependence on God, his grace, his faithfulness and the resource of love and joy he fills us with each day.
- The first finger, so often used for pointing, is about direction – we are called to know and embrace God's purposes for our lives and this prayer sets a direction for our day.
- The second finger is the tallest and speaks of strength – we can do all things through Christ and only through him, so we lay aside our strife and stress and believe this powerful truth that will bring us peace and power.
- The third finger – in many cultures the wedding finger – speaks of closeness, intimacy and the promise of God's Holy Spirit within us: he is faithful to speak to us, let us be faithful to listen.
- The little finger can remind us of what James has to say about the tongue, that even though it is one of the smallest parts of the body, it is capable of steering the whole course of your life like a rudder: so be full of praise, thanksgiving, faith and words of life to others.

> **Thumb**: Thank you Lord that your mercies are new every morning. Thank you that you're here with me now, filling me again to overflowing with your love; your joy; your peace; your patience; your goodness. May I live this day dependant on your presence with me.
>
> **First finger:** Thank you that you are here to guide my steps today. I set myself to keep in your rhythm of peace. I needn't rush or stress. I receive from you, this very moment, all the strength and energy I need in my mind and body for today.

Tallest finger: Thank you that I can do all things in Christ who strengthens me. Thank you that you have called me to live for you and serve others. Make me a channel of your blessing to everyone I come into contact with today.

Wedding finger: Thank you Lord that your Spirit is within me, guiding me today into all wisdom and truth. Please speak to me today, I am listening.

Little finger: Thank you Lord for giving me a voice to praise you. You fill my heart with joy and thanksgiving and my mouth with your praise and words of life! May my words this day bring honour to you and life to those around me.

Amy Roche[57]

Photoshop prayers

Is there a particular place or community God has called you to pray for? Can you walk its streets? Why not take a camera and ask God by his spirit to show you things that matter to him: aspects that can fuel your prayers. Use the images to create a structure for your prayers: praying for each as you are reminded of what God said to you.

If it's not moving, map it!

Do you have maps of your local town, nation or continent, of the places where the people God has asked you to pray for live? Use them to focus your prayers. Imagine the changes you are longing for sweeping across the terrain that lies before you. Pray with God's eye-view and ask him to let his compassion fill your heart.

Wax and wick

If you have a regular place of prayer and it is safe, have a candle that you light each time you pray. At intervals during your praying, stop and watch the flame. See the smoke rising from it and picture your prayers as incense rising to the throne of God.

Cosy corner

Create a corner of the room you most often pray in and make it a place of focussed prayer. Have space to kneel, sit or stand. Are there images or icons that inspire you to pray? Arrange them there. Keep close by the resources that help you pray – pictures of people you are committed to; maps and information; the journal you write in or pad you draw on; a Bible; other devotional books. Make these things that live in this space – things you don't use elsewhere – so that they become the furniture of your praying, the familiar symbols that enthuse you every time you turn to prayer.

Prayerhouse

If you are part of a local church or a group that meets together, set up a Prayerhouse – a dedicated space in which you can gather alone or in groups to pray. In our church we emptied a store cupboard and created a space that nobody needed for office or meetings: it has been a dedicated Prayerhouse for two years now. We used chalkboards, lining paper and cheap Ikea furnishings to kit it out. This can be a venue for 24/7 prayer weeks when you have them . . . but try to have it available permanently, then look for creative ways to use it! If you can, keep things that people write or create in prayer to inspire the prayers of others. Freshen the venue up every now and then. Fill it with loads of ideas and resources, so that whoever comes to pray will be inspired. Ask people to take their shoes off or in some other way mark it as holy ground.

Make collages of prayer needs; frame poems and readings; use mirrors; have bread and wine available; have Bibles around the place. Have a CD or MP3 player available with headphones. If many of the people who come to the Prayerhouse are likely to be unfamiliar with this way of praying, write some brief guidelines for the different activities and resources you have available. Laminate a Prayerhouse guide with some simple steps for getting started. If you have creative people in your group encourage them to get involved: but challenge them to pray first and create second.

Prayerstones

If there is a particular need you know you mustn't forget to pray about – perhaps someone is sick and you have been asked to join others in praying for them – use a prayerstone. Find a single stone or pebble and dedicate it to God as a symbol of the need you have before you. Paint a name or situation on the stone. Take an initial time to pray whilst holding the stone so that its feel and weight come to symbolize for you the situation you are praying for, then put it in your pocket (the one with your money in) and pray every time you touch it. If it is a small stone and a big need, put it in your shoe – you might have an uncomfortable day, but you certainly won't forget to pray.

Blessing

May the gifts that God has buried in your soul
Be fuel
For the fire of the Spirit
Treasure
For the temple of your God
Colours
For the collage of your worship

May the love that he has sown in you
Bear fruit in words
That work like wonders in your worries
In songs that sing the wounded into safety
In canvasses that capture God's true rainbow
In moments gluing broken hearts to freedom
In space that breaks the tyranny of fear

May the passion God has for you
Find a mirror
In a heart
Unafraid to receive him
In a mind unembarrassed to know him
In a body unashamed to embrace him
In a life undone enough to give him room

May your hopes be a home for him
And your imaginings invite him
May your dreams declare
His presence with you
And your poems paint his praise
May his will be your wallpaper
And his worship your window on the world
And may the music of your heart
Be his heart beating

And on this road of liberation
On your journey into wholeness
On the pathways of his promises
In the wanderings of your freedom
May God, your God,
Tabernacle with you

Gerard Kelly

RECIPROCAL

Licensed to Listen

O Lord God, Creator of all. Open my eye to beauty. Open
my mind to wonder.
Open my ears to others. Open my heart to you.

David Adam

The simple truth is if we want people to listen to us, we
have to listen to them first. People listen to people who
listen.

Bill Muir[58]

In her book T*he Wild Gospel: an Exploration of the
Transformation That Comes to a Life Surrendered to Christ*,
Alison Morgan describes hearing the story of Argentine
convert Hector Giminez

> By the age of 18 Hector was, in his own words, a drug
> addicted delinquent, wanted by the police and a dis-
> grace to his family. Shot while committing a crime, he
> was taken by his brother to a clinic where a nurse read
> the words of 2 Corinthians 5.17 to him: 'if any man is in
> Christ he is a new creation', and asked whether he wan-
> ted God to change his life. He said he did. They prayed
> and she left the room. Instantly the bleeding stopped

and the craving for drugs left him. Hector, still with two bullets in his body, joined the church and began to work with drug addicts and young people. He became a pastor, and within a year he had a congregation of a thousand. By 1995, after an astonishing story of radio broadcasts and crowded stadium meetings, he had a Sunday congregation of 15,000, a daily ministry to 10,000 people of whom two to three hundred respond to the gospel each day for the first time, and a network of 100 new churches. At that point, aged about 40, he came to England to tell his story. I listened to this man every day for a week; and the most striking thing he said, repeated over and over again throughout his talks, was the single phrase, *and the Lord said to me 'Hector'* . . . His whole life and ministry was sustained by the simple fact that he heard the Word of God.[59]

Hearing God; knowing that your Creator knows your name; being sure of what God says to you; recognizing his voice; experiencing a life of prayer that is interlaced with the gentle whisper of God: these sound as if they should describe the normal Christian life. But for the vast majority of us, they do not. Taking time to be with God, that is one battle. Telling God my troubles; remembering to pray for others; sharing my deepest dreams and longings with the Christ who walks by my side – none of these is easy to achieve, but they are at least achievable. But hearing God's voice: this surely is reserved for super-saints?

It would be tempting to say yes and avoid the hard work of bridging the gap between our aspirations and our actual experience: but to do so would not do justice to the biblical view of prayer. According to Scripture, God wants to speak to us. According to the lives of those described in Scripture's pages, he *does* speak to us. From

Adam and Eve via Abraham and Moses to Mary, Joseph, Paul, Ananias and Philip – and with a thousand others in between – hearing God seems to be a minimum qualification for even being mentioned in the Bible. The Bible is a record, generation after generation, of conversations with God. And no one pattern or technique is offered. God speaks, it seems, in many voices. Moses climbs a mountain to talk face to face with Yahweh; Elijah hears his whisper in a cave; Mary dreams; Peter falls into a trance; Paul is struck blind and hears God speak to him through Ananias; Philip finds his body picked up like a chess piece and moved to stand beside a stranger's chariot and God says, 'Go and talk to him'; John takes time out in his exile to seek God and gets simultaneous sound and vision theatre in a widescreen presentation of the history of the future. The word we use for this last experience, *revelation*, is the only word we can use to do justice to *all* of these experiences. They are all different – some quiet, some loud; some asleep, some awake; some verbal, some visual; some sought after, some entirely unexpected – but they do have this in common: when God speaks something is *revealed*. The only conclusion to be drawn from the sum of these experiences (and the full list of divine exchanges covered by the Bible would take a lot more words than this to describe) is that the God portrayed in the Bible is a God of revelation: he chooses to reveal himself to us. God has something to say and we are his intended audience.

Listen up

So Hector Giminez is describing a condition that *can* be the normal Christian experience, even if for many of us it isn't. The thought that God might know and use my

name and that my conversation with him can be dialogue not monologue; that I can hear and understand his
words to me: all this is part of the experience that awaits
me as I grow in prayer. If there is work to be done in har-
nessing my every creative gift and inspiration to build a
tabernacle worthy of the designer, then a further area in
which I am called to work as I grow in prayer is in the
tough task of *learning to listen*. The relationship into
which I am invited is reciprocal. God not only hears the
deepest longings of my heart – he invites me to hear his.

Canadian church leader Andrew Hawkins describes
the poverty that many of us experience in this area and
the importance of recovering listening as an element of
prayer

> . . . in twenty-three years of being a pastor I have found
> many people frustrated or guilt-ridden about their
> inability to communicate with God (pray). We all know
> that prayer anchors our spirituality and yet having reg-
> ular dynamic communion with God challenges us to the
> core. Prayer consists of a two-way conversation and
> what we have to say is not the most exciting part. Unless
> we contact God and sense him speaking to us, prayer
> bores us. What could be duller than closing your eyes
> and speaking out into the air? Our devotional life ends
> up on life-support.[60]

Out of this sense of frustration and need, Hawkins' book
*Whispers that Delight: Building a Listening-Centred Prayer
Life*, re-emphasizes listening as the very heart of prayer. In
common with Christian thinkers over many generations,
Hawkins has understood that without listening, prayer is
an empty activity. If the conversation of prayer moves in
one direction only, it will soon lose its energy and is likely over time to descend into a dutiful but unrewarding

ritual: endlessly repeated words mumbled to an indifferent deity who, somewhere beyond the ceiling, may or may not be listening. If you have ever asked or been asked the question 'Does God really hear my prayers?' you will know the frustration of this one-way experience. Even in human relationships, we would not tolerate such indifference for long. Therapists learn 'active listening' as a way of letting a client know, as they tell their story, that they are truly heard. Nodding and grunting and making eye contact are all used to affirm the speaker. No wonder, then, that we fail to value prayer if we've never even heard God grunt. Each time we return to prayer, we will do so with a heavy heart, forced *yet again* to bare our soul to an apparently indifferent listener, who can't even be bothered to acknowledge our presence.

But what if this was not how prayer was meant to be? What if we were called instead into an active conversation in which our presence is acknowledged and our contribution valued; in which the words we pour out from our heart are *heard* and, better still, responded to? What if there really is someone on the other end of the line? Might not prayer then become a great adventure? Might we not run to our place of prayer, eager to find out what our conversation partner has to tell us today? Like Sergeant Lewis probing the mighty brain of Morse, might we not marvel at the wisdom with which the mysteries of our lives are unravelled and come each day with more clues to be pored over together? 'What is our life on earth', asks Carlo Carretto, 'if not discovering, becoming conscious of, penetrating, contemplating, accepting, loving this mystery of God, the unique reality which surrounds us, and in which we are immersed like meteorites in space?'

Here is a vision for our life of prayer that refuses to throw darts of indifference at a wall of uncaring, impersonal coldness, that wants instead to dive into a real conversation. The difference lies in listening.

Rocket fuel

Through reading the works of those who have gone deeply into prayer over many centuries, talking with those engaged in that same adventure today and examining our own experience, we have come to the conclusion that listening is the rocket fuel of prayer. You can pray without listening but the weight is enormous: you will be pushing a vehicle designed to be driven. Once you hear the voice on the other end of the line, though, motivation comes; energy is sparked: the whole nature of the activity changes. Listening ignites prayer. It is in hearing God that the adventure of prayer takes off. Yet this is so poorly understood and taught in our churches that many find prayer a chore. How do we hear God's voice? How do we develop as listeners? What will *learning to listen* look like?

Richard Foster tells the story of Phoebe Palmer, a pioneer theologian and philanthropist in nineteenth century New York. Phoebe was mother to six children, but lost three in their very early years to different tragedies. The third of these, Eliza, was killed when a dropped oil lamp engulfed her cot in flames. Out of this tragedy, racked with grief, Phoebe turned to prayer. If ever she needed to hear the voice of God, this was the time. Here is her account of the 'prayer conversation' that ensued

> While pacing the room, crying to God, amid the tumult of grief, my mind was arrested by a gentle whisper, saying 'Your Heavenly Father loves you. He would not permit such a great trial, without intending that some great

good proportionate in magnitude and weight should result.' . . . In the agony of my soul I had exclaimed 'O. what shall I do!'And the answer now came, 'Be still and know that I am God.' I took up the precious Word and cried, 'O teach me the lessons of this trial', and the first lines to catch my eye on opening the Bible were these, 'O the depths of the riches, both of the wisdom and knowledge of God! How unsearchable are his judgments and his ways past finding out!' . . . The tumult of feeling was hush . . . 'What thou knowest not now, thou shalt know hereafter', was assuringly whispered. Wholly subdued before the Lord, my chastened spirit nestled in quietness under the wing of the Holy Comforter . . .'[62]

Whilst no single incident will capture perfectly the lessons to be learned in listening to God, this powerful passage does contain many of the key ingredients to be aware of. It illustrates at least three of the primary ways in which God speaks to us – through the 'inner whisper', the witness of his Spirit with our spirit; through bringing to our minds things we have already heard from him, but need now; and through guiding us into Scripture, the depository of his recorded voice over centuries.

Phoebe Palmer talks almost with ease of hearing the whisper of God. His answer to her questions come almost before they are uttered: but this is someone who has learned to recognize his voice, who has grown in prayer to the place where dialogue, not monologue, is the norm. This points to two principles that are at the heart of listening prayer.

- **You can become tuned to the inner voice of God**. Like Phoebe Palmer, you can come to a place where you can say with confidence that you have heard God's whisper. We know from experience that for many people this is not the norm. But we know from Scripture and life that it is possible. Our response must be to make this a goal: to aspire to a grasp on prayer in which our ears are as active as our tongues. Will you commit to an understanding of prayer that includes listening and join God in the adventure of bringing that understanding into your experience?

- **Coming to this place takes time and trouble**. In any relationship, it takes time to truly know each other so that we truly hear each other and in our life of prayer there are added complications: God is Spirit not body; he is not in the room in the same sense that the chair is in the room; his voice to us is an inner voice, not an audible voice; hearing God's voice involves quieting the many other voices that clamour for attention. Listening to God involves both *training* and *tuning* and neither of these will come without a commitment of *time*.

It is also notable in Phoebe Palmer's account that her sense of God's word to her begins with remembering her knowledge of his love for her. God is reminding her of what she knows already. This pattern is evident throughout the scriptural record and it seems that God's purpose in speaking to us is often to remind us of the things we have forgotten: that he loves us and has a plan for each of us; that he can be trusted; that he is at work in our world; that he will not leave us. These are not religious clichés trotted out to console us – they are deep truths about God and he reminds us of them because we forget them. Here then is a third and fourth principle of listening to the voice of God

- **God is always true to his own nature**. The things he tells you today will resonate with the things he has told you already. His purpose in speaking to you is to reveal himself to you and he does so in radical consistency with his own nature. The foundational revelation of God in the Jewish faith is the declaration to Moses 'I am who I am' (Ex. 3:14). This complex grammatical construction has many meanings and recent scholars have seen in it a statement of the reliability of the character of God.

- **It is in God's nature to respond**. The notion that God is impassive and unmoved by the events of our lives is false. Scripture shows us a God who is alive to our cry, ready to respond to us in love. As Walter Brueggemann shows us, this is the very heart of the Exodus story – the foundational narrative of the Jewish and Christian faiths: 'The wonder of the narrative is that the cry from below evoked the power of God from above. In response to the slave cry, God moved the darkness and the sea, God mobilized creation on behalf of the needy slaves, God managed the chaos redemptively. They were freed, as they never expected to be!'[63] God is always true to his character and his character is responsive to us. Our God does not offer us a recording message suggesting we call back later. He does not leave us hanging on a busy signal. He picks up. He is the Liberator, the Warrior, the one who *hears* and *answers* our call.

Lastly, our brief insight into the prayer life of Phoebe Palmer also illustrates the central role of Scripture in God's self-revelation. We will explore the relationship of Scripture to prayer more fully in the following chapter, but it is vital here that we understand that the Bible is one of the most significant tools that God will use in speaking to us and that the things he brings to us by other means will *resonate* with this, his long-term journal. Scripture is important to us for many reasons, but central among these is that it *lets us know who God is*. We discover God in our experience and we get to know him in prayer, but the Bible is the backbone of this journey and the more we let it speak to us, the more fluently and freely we will recognize God's voice. Two simple principles help us to put Scripture at the very centre of our listening

- **God will speak to us through his written word.** The Holy Spirit is alive in us and brings God's life to us: and he also brings to life *for us* the words of Scripture. It is not true to say that the Bible is the *only* means by which God speaks, but it is a *primary* means. This is not a 'Protestant' obsession: adventurers in prayer from every branch of the church have discovered, over many years, that it is an indispensable means. Build the Bible into your life of prayer; expect God to speak to you through it; invite the Holy Spirit to open your eyes to it and you will soon find a change to your experience of the silence of God.

- **Knowing how God speaks within Scripture helps us to know how he speaks outside of it.** As you move deeper into the apprenticeship of prayer, you will begin to see that the Bible is, among other things, a notebook of the discoveries of earlier apprentices. From the very beginning of God's dealings with men and women, the Bible has captured snatches of conversation, stories and prayers, accounts of what it is like doing business with this God. The deeper you know Scripture, the more easily you will recognize his voice in your life. The more you hold up Scripture alongside your experience, the better you will be able to understand that experience.

Speak to me

God will speak to you through an inner voice enlivened by his Spirit and he will speak to you through Scripture, but as you grow in listening to God, you will discover some of the other ways in which he speaks to you. Consistent with his character and resonating with Scripture, God's voice can come to us in many other ways

- Exceptionally, God may speak to you in an audible voice. This *is* unusual, but it is not impossible. Our good friend Helen Santos met God in this way. Her daughter had already come to faith, but Helen herself, raised a Catholic, had become a Buddhist and had no sympathy for this 'Jesus' experience and talk of being 'converted.' She gave her daughter quite a hard time for several months. And then one day, walking across the park in front of the Royal Crescent in Bath, she heard an audible voice that asked her, just had it had once asked St Paul, 'Helen, why are you resisting me?'
- More often, God will speak to you by helping you to understand the things you see. Like a tourist guide pointing out to his group the wonders around them, God will say to you 'Let me show you something . . .' He may ask you 'What does this mean to you? What do you think of this?' On occasions, when walking and praying, we have been so aware of God speaking to us through the things we see around us that we have taken a series of photographs. Looking

over them later, we have been more able to see the thread of God's voice to us. People and places, signs and symbols and the wonders of the natural world can all speak to us. Francis Collins, one of the world's most significant genetic scientists, came to faith because he came across a waterfall that fell into three distinct streams. God spoke to him through it and the reality of the Trinity became a foundation of his faith.

- Lastly, God will speak to you through the words and experiences of others. There are living friends whose voices can become to you the voice of God and there are distant friends, alive and gone, whose writings can speak powerfully to you. The key in hearing God through others is to set their words alongside both Scripture and the inner witness of the Spirit and to learn who you can trust. When God has spoken to you clearly and powerfully through someone, it is quite possible that he may do so again. Learn to trust those who have shown themselves worthy of your trust and God's.

In all these areas, three principles remain true

- The different ways by which God speaks to us will serve to confirm each other. Many voices are more solid than one isolated claim.
- The ultimate test of how well you are hearing is what happens. God's words are never words alone: they are intimately related to actions and events in the real world. Sometimes it takes time to see how accurate your grasp on God's word to you has been.
- God's pace and perspective are very different from yours. God will always speak to you from his

perspective, not from yours. You may want to know, by next Tuesday, the precise answer to a very specific question. God may want to speak to you about something entirely different, something that matters to him but has hardly registered with you. The more you get used to hearing God, the more often you will see that he always gives the right answer but that we tend very often to ask the wrong question. Stephen Gaukroger points out that the road to knowing God's will for our lives is a long one, it involves hearing God many times, slowly bringing our plans and projects into lines with his purposes

We often imagine that guidance comes easily to Christian workers. Don't they all have a hot line to heaven telling them where to work, when, and how to get there? Actually they are often as confused as we are! David Livingstone first thought God was calling him to China – and then went to Africa. William Carey felt he should serve God in Tahiti – and ended up in India. And as for Thomas Barnardo – he felt sure that God wanted him in China. He had come from Dublin to London to train as a missionary doctor. While in preparation to go he started a meeting for 'street-children' in the East End of London. After one of these meetings one of the poorest of the boys simply would not go home. Jim Jarvis told Barnardo that he had no home to go to! Barnardo could hardly believe it. Soon after this he met Lord Shaftesbury at a dinner party and told him about the homelessness and poverty in the East End. Anthony Shaftesbury did not believe him until he was taken by Barnardo himself to a warehouse in Whitechapel. Here he encountered seventy-three boys living rough! 'Are you sure that it is to China God is sending you?' Something 'clicked' inside Thomas

Barnardo and he devoted his life to the needy in London instead of China. This happened in 1866. In the thirty-nine years to his death his organization admitted 59,384 children to his homes and helped a quarter of a million others.'[64]

Long haul listening

Listening to God, then, is for the long haul. There is a lifetimes worth of learning in this one key task of coming to know his voice. More than anything, learning to hear God is about getting to know God. You recognize and respond to God's voice in exactly the way a child will hear a parent, even in a noisy crowd. As you come to know God better you come to recognize the patterns by which he works in your life and the lives of others and you know his character from Scripture and history and the many, many ways he has proved himself to you. Through all this, over time, you become confident in recognizing his voice. There is no voice-recognition software you can buy to be sure when God is speaking. You just have to get to know him. Jim Borst, author of the excellent booklet *Coming to God in the Stillness*, says

No words can describe, no book explain, what it means to love Jesus. We can only know from personal experience. When he visits our heart, it is bathed in the light of truth . . . Those who have tasted Jesus hunger for more. Those who have drunk of him are thirsty for more. But only those who love him are able to fulfil their desires – to know joy in his embrace now and glory later in his kingdom.[65]

Psychologists who don't believe in God will tell you that in all the above techniques you are merely listening to yourself. And to some degree they are right, because the *you* that is most at home in talking to God is the true *you* – the deep you hidden below the layers of behaviours and protections you have built and learned. Part of learning to hear God *is* learning to hear yourself. It is only when you let your deepest self speak that God's replies make sense and the battle to recognise your own true voice is a stage on the journey to hearing God's. You should not be afraid to let the journey of prayer take you deeper into your own heart. As Evelyn Underhill writes, '. . . worship, though the whole man of sense and spirit, feeling, thought, and will, is and must be truly concerned in it, is above all the work of that mysterious 'ground' of our being, that sacred hearth of personality, where the created spirit of man adheres to the increate Spirit of God.'[66]

The very definition of this conversation is captured by the psalmists who says that 'deep calls to deep' (Ps. 42:8). But it is not true to say that only your voice is active in this conversation. You were created by a loving God who shaped your very soul and has left his fingerprints all over your life. When you call, he will answer. The pattern of his voice is known to you deep, deep in the part of you where being his creature – a *created being* – is your greatest joy. You are Adam, you are Eve and he is the one who walks in the garden calling out 'Where are you?' To find him; to hear his voice; to answer is to release and respond to the deepest longing of your very being. It is to remember who you are. It is to come home.

One last area is worth exploring before we leave the question of listening to God. As you spend time in the presence of God, as you become attuned to his voice and learn to hear his words, you will find that he gives you eyes to see and ears to hear the sufferings of the world around you. Just as God listens to us, he asks us to listen to our neighbour. Just as he responds to our cry, he asks us to respond. By spending time with God we become more like him and a listening God will shape us into listening people. The apprentice who learns to hear the whisper of God in the silence of prayer will soon learn to hear that same whisper in the clamour of a broken world.

Our times with God will teach us 'to listen with all our faculties to the messages sounding out from the world around us. They can be heard through our physical environment, the media, conversations and life encounters with others and as we listen to the turmoil that can be within our own spirits.'[67] Bishop Peter Price writes on the place of 'small Christian communities' as a transforming presence in their cultures and insists that the *authentic* voice of God is heard when three distinct threads are in place: 'listening to the daily reality of local life, to the shared life of the small Christian community and reflection upon both in the light of the Bible.'[68] Similarly, many years ago the German pastor Dietrich Bonhoeffer called his fellow leaders to a ministry of listening. 'We should listen with the ears of God that we may speak the Word of God', he wrote. 'Christians, especially ministers, so often think they must always contribute something when they are in the company of others, that this is the one service they have to render. They forget that listening can be a greater service than speaking.'[69]

Exercises

Engage the Equalizer

To tune in to God you need to tune out other voices. You need silence into which God can speak. This means two things: time and space. Before you can even begin the journey of adding listening to your life of prayer, you need to get practical. *When* exactly will you listen for God's voice and *where* exactly will you hear it? When might you be able to come to God in the stillness? Allocate a time when you will be free of interruptions and decide where this should happen. Lastly, in preparation for this journey, list the 'other voices' most likely to distract you. They are different for all of us: yours might be the mobile phone or MP3 player, the people you live with, the TV or radio. You might find crowded places difficult or shop windows distracting. Try to analyse just which voices most often interrupt your silence and make a commitment to break their power. Whatever you have to do to silence competing voices and find space to be still before God, do it – and then find a way to do it much more often.

Lean into listening

Not everyone is going to benefit from trying, right away, to be still before God for hours at a time. Prayer is not a Porsche that moves from nought to sixty in a few seconds. Wisdom says 'Build up slowly.' There is grace and growth in gradual acceleration. Start with a commitment to place pauses in your prayers. Every few moments in your prayer, simply stop in silence and ask God to speak to you. If and when you find this helping you, make the pauses longer and the prayers shorter. Remember to thank God for the things he says to you. Keep a journal if it helps you remember. When you read Scripture, make it your habit to pause in silence for just thirty seconds before you read, asking God to speak to you. Make the thirty seconds sixty and the sixty, 120, until you find yourself able to wait on God for longer periods. Add the same pause moments *after* reading, letting the words you have read sink deeply into your spirit. Try to get to a place where your listening outweighs speaking in your prayer habits, to match the design of your head: you have two ears and only one tongue. Don't treat this as law, treat it as learning and adventure. Commit the process to God. Talk to him about it. Ask for his help. See if he has anything to say to you about it. As you commit to learning to listen – listen.

Put ears to your eyes

When you are next walking and praying at the same time, ask God specifically if there is anything you see through which he wants you to *hear*. We have known God speak powerfully to us through pub signs; the names on trucks; road signs ('No entry' was a repeated and particularly powerful lesson); a sculptor working in her garden; a series of unfinished buildings; the sight of boats entering and leaving a harbour. Each of these became a vehicle for important words God wanted us to hear and in each case we had asked specifically that God would speak. What might there be, in the thousand sights that greet your eyes each day, that God can use to speak his word to you?

Be prepared for the prophetic

Prophecy is a very important gift in Scripture. God speaks to people through people. Let God know that you are open to hearing him through his trusted servants. Watch who he brings your way and be willing to weigh up their words . . .

A Russian Prayer

You alone are God eternal,
uncreated,
O Holy Trinity, Father, Son and Spirit,
Creator of all that is seen and unseen!

You are Lord and Master.
You have wounded me
with your love
and transformed me.
You have captured me
with your beauty
and I am transfixed,

O Trinity, my God!
There are Three,
and the features of each are one,
for the Three are One countenance,
O my God,
who are God of the whole universe!
Let my eyes see your glory,
for it is that which I announce
in words every day
Creator and Master of all Ages,
O Holy Trinity, my God!

St Seraphim of Sarov[70]

Blessing

In the silence of your soul
May his voice reach you
In the cracks
Where you are broken
In the pits
Where you sink low
In the tangled web of weeds
That choke your dreams
In the bitter sharp-edged stones
That pierce your feet
In your flaws and in your failings
In your fears
May you hear him

May you come to know the tone
Of his affection
And recognize the accents
Of his love
May his prose
Become your reading
And his poetry
Your song
May his marvels be the mine
Your mind is sourced in
His magnificence the spring
Your streams flow from
In your listening and in your longings
In your life
May you hear him

Gerard Kelly

Watch

From my earliest childhood I had been taught to wait on the Lord – to look to the one who brought his people out of slavery in Egypt and brought them to this promised land of Israel. Peace and plenty were his promises to us. But I often wondered – did he hear us at all? Our land was occupied by the armies of Rome. Our freedoms were taken from us. The taxes we paid served only to make our enemies stronger and increase the hold they had on us.

We were slaves once more – not in Egypt but in the very land our God had given to us.

And our God, it seemed, said nothing. For four hundred years no prophet had arisen to speak hope to our people. The dream of freedom; the promise that Messiah would come; the longing for the great day of the Lord – all these were fading from our lives. We remembered. We hoped. We prayed: but often I would ask myself, where is the God of the Exodus now?

But all that was before the angels came: before Heaven opened and God spoke to me. And I knew, the night the angel first came to me, that the silence of the skies was broken. Four hundred years we waited and when at last God spoke – joy of joys – it was to me.

I was so young then, I knew so little of the world and its ways but I did know one thing. I knew what it was to hear the voice of God.

And I heard him speak my name. Mary . . .

I didn't know how to respond to what I'd heard. How could I? This was news that no girl had ever received before. It spoke of an event that had never before happened.

But there was one thing I did know: behind this mystery, my God was at work. We had waited so long for the Lord to come to us, to speak to us, to end our exile. There had been so many promises, so many mysteries that the prophets had left to us. There had been so many days and nights under the silence of Heaven: our questions unanswered, our longings unfulfilled.

And now God was speaking – sending angels, working wonders entering the quiet expectancy of our ordinary lives. Even my cousin Elizabeth had received the news she had despaired of ever hearing. To be with child, after giving up hope: what a miracle of grace this was. And for me, to hear such things about my own destiny.

What could I do but worship? How could I respond but to praise the God who does not forget his people? I didn't know what would become of me, how all this would unfold. But how could I not trust him, this God who always loves the humble poor?

For thirty years I waited to see what would become of the strange promises I heard in those weeks. I remembered every detail, every moment as I watched Jesus grow. In fear for his life, we fled to Egypt and Joseph built his business there. It would be seven years before we could return in safety.

Even then, Jesus made no move to reveal himself. There were signs, of course, but only I saw them, because only I was looking. As far as everyone else was concerned, he was Jesus, son of Joseph: a carpenter apprenticed to the family firm.

But then the day came when he told me he must leave and I knew this was at last the time.

He was gone for almost six weeks. He took nothing with him: neither food nor extra clothing. I had no idea where he was, only that he had been to talk to his cousin, John. And when he stood once more in our home, I knew that everything had changed and that he would leave me. There was a look in his eye that brought a chill to my soul. But I knew what it meant and that I had once again to accept the will of one whose thoughts were high above my own.

We went as normal to the synagogue that week. I was sitting with the women when I saw that he had risen from his *place to read the Scriptures. I could hardly breathe as he opened the scroll. For a few moments in the silence of eternity, only I knew that he was about to announce his mission. When this is over, I told myself, they will all know.*

And when I heard the words he read and what he had to say about them, I knew that every promise I had heard would be fulfilled. And that the moment was now.

Why watch?

The story of Mary is beautifully illustrative of the life we enjoy in communion with God. Mary is devout and perfectly represents the believer who both speaks to and hears from God. But that is not all that happens in this one young life. Mary also represents for us a third truth, without which neither her story nor the salvation of the world would be complete: God is at work in the world. Here is no divine watchmaker, winding up the universe and setting it on its way: this Creator is active in his creation. Mary does speak to God and she does hear from God: but after speaking and hearing, she is invited to watch as God works. She sees and feels the growth of a child in her womb; she experiences his birth; she looks on as shepherds and kings come to honour him; she hears strange words, sees unexpected things. She watches him grow through childhood into manhood.

In the midst of all the miracles and mayhem of the stable scene, we are told that 'the shepherds told everyone what had happened and what the angel had said to them about this child. All who heard the shepherds' story were astonished, but Mary quietly treasured these things in her heart and thought about them often' (Lk. 2:17–19). She was a watcher. Promises had been made, prophecies delivered. God was on the move to save his people and Mary *watched* to see how he would do it. Hearing God's word, for her, was preliminary to seeing him work. The word of faith is not an end in itself: it is an invitation to see faith fulfilled.

And so it is in our own lives of prayer. We *are* invited to speak to God. We *are* invited to hear God speak to us and beyond speaking and hearing, we are invited to *see God at work*. Watching what God does is part of our apprenticeship. God reveals his character not only through his words but through his works. In my heart and my world, the traces of God's fingerprints are clues to who he is and how he loves me. Watching him at work is part of learning who he is. The declaration to Moses 'I am who I am' (Ex. 3:14) also has the meaning 'I will be who I will be' and may carry the implication 'You will know who I am by what I do.' God's actions are utterly consistent with God's nature: we can read the Exodus text as dialogue: Moses asked 'Who are you?' and God says 'Let me show you.'

It is not enough to say that God's actions *prove* his word to us – they are part of his word to us. In the ongoing conversation with God that is our life of prayer, his actions in our lives and in our world are part of the dialogue. 'Watch me', he says, 'because if you listen but don't watch you won't get the full picture.' 'Watch carefully. There are things you need to see.' 'There are things you shouldn't miss.' 'Let me show you.'

ROOTED

Soaked in Scripture

God is 'the Truth.' The Bible is the 'truth about the
Truth.' Theology is the 'the truth about the truth about
the Truth.'

Richard Wurmbrand[71]

Christians feed on Scripture. Holy Scriptures nurture the
holy community as food nurtures the human body.
Christians don't simply learn or study or use Scripture;
we assimilate it, take it into our lives in such a way that
it gets metabolized into acts of love, cups of cold water,
missions into all the world, healing and evangelism and
justice in Jesus' name, hands raised in adoration of the
Father, feet washed in company with the Son.

Eugene Peterson[72]

Among leaders of the Western church, Richard Foster
has been a pioneer for over three decades of the call to a
deeper life of prayer. His books, including *Celebration of
Discipline* and *Prayer: Finding the Heart's True Home* have
achieved classic status for many people and the network
he has founded, Renovare, has introduced believers
from diverse denominational backgrounds to the six
great schools of spirituality by which Christian history

has been shaped. You will find Foster's material quoted in many books on prayer and you will meet Christians all over the world who have been inspired and influenced by his ministry. In recent years, that ministry has found a new passion and strength of purpose in encouraging all who seek a deeper life with God to read the Bible. *The Spiritual Formation Bible* is a new translation with notes and reflections on the life of prayer, bringing together the input of scholars and spiritual teachers across a wide spectrum of the church. Foster's most recent book *Life with God* explores the role of Scripture in discipleship and growth. Co-written with Kathryn A. Helmers, *Life with God* asserts that all the great schools of Christian spiritual formation find their ultimate source in the Bible

> The Bible is all about human life 'with God.' It is about how God has made this 'with' life possible and will bring it to pass. In fact the name *Immanuel*, meaning 'God with us', is the title given to the one and only Redeemer because it refers to God's everlasting intent for human life – namely, that we should be in every aspect a dwelling place for God. Indeed the unity of the Bible is discovered in the development of life 'with God' as a reality on earth, centred in the person of Jesus. We might call this *The Immanuel Principle of Life* . . . From Genesis to Revelation we learn that the Immanuel Principle . . . alone serves to guide human life aright on earth now and even illuminates the future of the universe. It is the wellspring of the river of life flowing through the Bible, surging with the gracious word of God to all humankind – '*I am with you.*' This river pours into the thirsty wastelands of the human soul, inviting us to enter with its insistent call, 'Will you be *with* Me?'[73]

The Immanuel Principle suggests not only that the Bible can be central to your intimacy with God, but that your intimacy with God is central to the Bible. The lessons you are learning in the Jesus school of prayer; the challenges you meet and overcome in your apprenticeship; the journey to a deeper with-God life: all these *are* what the Bible is about. Where you are heading is where the Bible lands. These are two distinct avenues of God's work in your life

- The stirrings of his Spirit within you, in which deep calls to deep and the Son of Man calls you to walk with him and work with him and watch what he is doing: wooing you into intimacy with the Father.
- The revelation in Scripture of who God is and what he plans to do with the planet he has made: repairing the broken bridges that have kept Creator and creation apart and diving once more into his world to 'make all things new.'

God's pas-de-deux

But they do not have two separate goals: they share the same purpose and the same destination – the union of creature and Creator. As you seek a deeper walk with God, you find that Scripture serves as your most vital resource. The Bible fuels your praying. And as you grow in prayer you find a new love for and grasp of God's written words and a new appreciation of his story. Praying fuels your reading of the Bible. Scripture drives you into prayer and prayer drives you into Scripture. This dynamic partnership, the *pas-de-deux* of the dance that is your life with God, means that you can't travel far at all on the pathways of prayer without embracing

Scripture's role. Life in the Jesus school of prayer becomes a *rooted* life: a life so soaked in the story that God's words begin to change you from the inside. Jesus points you to the Bible and in the Bible you meet Jesus. When you encounter the Bible at the heart of your with-God journey, Richard Foster asserts, you are 'coming to the text and seeing through the text, even beyond the text, to the Lord of the text.'[74] Scripture is the soil from which your life with God is fed. It is the source that fuels your growth. There is no more nutritious story into which to sink your roots.

In this partnership of Bible and prayer, there are three key ways in which our reading of Scripture can shape and change our prayers.

Firstly, Scripture brings focus. When I allow Scripture to inspire and inform my prayers, I am drawn into a more certain focus. By bringing the people and places I am praying about *alongside* those of the Bible, I am empowered to imagine just how the God of the Bible might want me to pray. The act of coming to Scripture to seek wisdom for now brings the past and future together, allowing me to tap into conceptual resources that are outside my personal context but are embedded in the history of God. The Bible is, above all, story: but it is not fiction. It is the story of God, the grand narrative through which we understand the care of the Creator for his creatures. When the Hebrew slaves came out of Egypt, propelled into freedom by the strange events of the first Passover, they were clearly told by Yahweh to remember this night (Ex. 12:11–17). Year by year and from generation to generation, they were to remember in the Passover supper the events by which their freedom was won. Through this family ritual, children born years after the events themselves would be invited to indwell the story and to relive for themselves the marvellous acts of God. And this repeated recitation becomes the basis, in turn, of Christian worship. Derek Tidball explains

> When the Jewish Passover meal today reaches the point at which the great acts of God have been recited, the leader urges the people on with these words: '*Then how much more, doubled and redoubled, is the claim the Omnipresent has upon our thankfulness.*' In view of the great accomplishments of the cross, how much more, doubled, trebled and quadrupled, is the claim the Christ, the Lord's Passover, has on our thankfulness![75]

Scripture allows us to enter into a history not our own in order to embrace a future yet to be revealed. We are born into a history that reaches back to the very birth of our tribe and will stretch forward into the immeasurable years of our future. By allowing our prayers to be soaked in this same story; by letting it inspire us; by aligning our longings with the hope it holds out to us; we bring our life of prayer into the very centre of God's purposes. God has not kept secret from us who he is or what he has in mind for us. Scripture allows us to embrace his open secret and, by prayer, to inch our way towards our part in it.

Secondly, Scripture offers keys for life and healing. Aligning our thoughts and dreams with the story of God also draws our lives, step by step, towards wholeness. Whether you are praying about obstacles to growth in your own life or praying for another, the truth will set you free. We have learned to take this very seriously and to pray specific words of Scripture over the areas we are struggling with. 'Praying Scripture' is a whole approach to intercessory prayer that allows you to pray for people in a vast range of situations, by finding the Scriptures that most clearly declare God's purposes and speaking them out in faith. This is not magic, nor is it the power of positive confession. It is simply a way of taking Jesus' most simple and compelling prayer 'May your Kingdom come soon. May your will be done here on earth, just as it is in heaven (Mt. 6:10, NLT) and applying it to specific situations. Gregory Boyd says of the Lord 's Prayer, 'This prayer, then, is a prayer for change and the change involves moving from a world in which the Father's name is not honoured, his will is not done and his rule not established, into a world in which these things are as they should be.'[76]

As we meditate on Scripture, we become more and more familiar with God's will for our world. As we meditate on the needs about which we are concerned, we become more and more aware of the places where God's will is not done. Prayer, in its simplest possible form, is the bringing together of the two. Praying the promises of Scripture in the face of the world's evident brokenness and our own is one way of entering into the brokenness of the heart of God and finding out what healing might look like. Amy Roche describes the role of Scripture in enabling her to identify and ultimately overcome limitations in her own grasp of God's purposes

> I've spent years looking at Scriptures that speak of grace and freedom: finding them; noting them; learning them; reciting them; praying them. I had a tendency early on in my Christian life to feel the need to earn God's favour – and most of the time I wasn't managing to do so! Looking back it's clear to me what unnecessary weight I carried all this time; feeling that I was constantly letting God down. I felt that I had failed to meet his standards, when in fact

they were all of my own making. But I discovered that 'the word of God is full of living power. It is sharper than the sharpest knife, cutting deep into our innermost thoughts and desires. It exposes us for what we are. I came to see that the Bible was telling me I am free from the law that brings condemnation and that I could live in the freedom of the grace of God. The Bible made me aware of the gap between my feelings and the truth: just like a knife separating bone from flesh. I knew that I needed a deeper, inner revelation about the grace of God. There's something God loves about a heart that is hungry enough to seek Him, to persevere and not give up in the areas of our lives that take time to be transformed. All the teaching I have heard, and books I have read have been an amazing help in the journey. But sometimes, too, I've known a moment when suddenly just reading a well-read, familiar few verses in the Bible has been like opening a door in my mind to let the light flood in and help me see something that before I couldn't.[77]

Thirdly, Scripture brings maturity and understanding to our prayers. The Bible, in a sense, *teaches us how to pray*. All too often our prayers are projections, simply reflecting our own immature understandings. As we read and inwardly digest the words of Scripture and allow our worldview to be shaped by them, our prayers in turn go deeper. We find ourselves praying according to God's will and in the process gaining a broader understanding of his purposes. The three-way process of considering Scripture, pondering our world and its problems and, somewhere between the two, soaking in the presence of God to hear his voice, gives us the best hope of seeing as he sees, the best route into a truly God-shaped worldview. Academic enquiry alone will not serve up a God's eye-view of the world, but study

submitted to Scripture and surrendered to the presence
of the Spirit just might.

What does God expect?

Jesus suggests 'love of God and neighbour' as a sum-
mary of the full demands of God's purposes for our
planet. What might this mean in your spheres of activity? Jesus himself offers these words. They are compre-
hensive. No matter what you spend your time doing
and no matter how distant it seems from the world of
the Bible, it sits squarely under the umbrella of this call
to active love. But it takes more than simple reading,
more than knowledge-acquisition, to see this. The Bible
must be read with the heart as well as the mind. This
takes considered thought, meditation, prayerful reading. It takes surrender to the Holy Spirit: heart, mind,
body and soul brought before God and offered as blank
slate on which to write. Without the piety of a surrendered heart, the power of Scripture to shape us is dimin-
ished. It is in the overlap of the avenues of God in our
lives, where prayer and Scripture meet, that we will
most see and hear the truths God has for us.

Divine reading

One way of bringing mind and heart together, of reading the Bible as a devotional exercise, is *Lectio divina*:
divine reading. An ancient Christian practice and central
to the 'rule' of many monastic communities, *Lectio divina*
is being rediscovered by many Christians in our day. It
is practised in the four steps traditionally referred to as
'the monks' ladder': reading, meditation, prayer and

contemplation. The steps are used in sequence, with the aim of both hearing God and responding to him. *Lectio divina* is a powerful tool in personal devotion because it combines Scripture with prayer and relies heavily on the felt presence of the Holy Spirit. The four steps can become a simple pattern of Read; Reflect; Respond; Rest: a repeated cycle by which we invite God to speak to us through his word; submit to his Spirit; surrender to his presence – and let the revelation that comes be the foundation and fuel of the prayers that follow.

- **Read**: Take a short passage of the Bible and read it aloud. As you read, listen out for the word or phrase that most directly speaks to you. Which part of the passage is the Holy Spirit most bringing to your attention?
- **Reflect**: Consider the word or phrase you have identified and repeat it several times. Reflect on the connections you find with your life and situation. Is there anything specific that God is saying to you through this word or phrase?
- **Respond**: Turn these thoughts and reflections into prayer, offering them back to God in response to his word to you. What comes to mind that you need to give thanks for or repent of? What will you ask of God in response to the word that has come to you? Commit yourself to follow through on the actions your reading points you towards.
- **Rest**: End your time of reflection in the stillness of contemplation. Rest in God's presence and his love for you. Enjoy his peace and make time for silence. In this place of rest, what is God revealing to you?

If you don't know where to start with letting Scripture shape your prayers, start by considering what the Bible has to say *about* prayer. Most of what we know and believe about prayer comes to us from Scripture and the examples it gives to us. Take passages where the Bible speaks about prayer or where specific prayers are recorded and use these as the basis for your meditations. Let Scripture itself shape your understanding of prayer.

Faith in the furnace

In 2006 Rob Lacey, author of *The Word On the Street* and *The Liberator* and founder of the Lacey Theatre Company, found himself fighting cancer for the third time in his life. Five years earlier he had come to the very threshold of death but had been healed. Now he was, once again, facing the worst possible prognosis. His wife Sandra was pregnant with their second child. His son Lukas was struggling to cope with a father once again brought down by sickness. Many of us prayed and fasted for Rob's healing, standing with him in his struggle.

What we found extraordinary, in the midst of great pain and trouble, was the faith with which Rob himself prayed. His trust in God was unbreakable. His willingness to stand against the death that was claiming his body cell-by-cell put to shame those of us watching from the safe terraces of our whole bodies. Spending time with Rob in what would prove to be the last weeks of his earthly life, we wondered 'Where does this faith come from? Where did Rob learn to pray like that?'

The answer is not hard to find. For five years Rob had 'lived in' Scripture. Performing *The Word on the Street* and researching and writing *The Liberator*, Rob had indwelt the words he was speaking and writing, getting under the skin of the text to ferret out its deeper meanings. You can't perform a script that hasn't taken up residence within you. Almost by accident, Rob learned to pray the way the Bible prays. He prayed to the God of Abraham, Isaac and Jacob, of Moses and David and Mary and, yes, of Lazarus. Standing with Shadrach, Meshach and Abednego at the sizzling edge of a furnace promising only extinction, he was able to say

> If we're chucked into this blazing oven, the God we work for could pull us out alive. He'll rescue us from your cruelty, King. Even if he doesn't and we fry, you should still know, there'd be no regrets – no way are we bowing down to your gods or your overgrown gold Action Man.[78]

The Bible taught Rob to pray. It changed his expectations and built his trust in God. It became the landscape in which he swam and ran. And the lessons he learned in that landscape changed the way he walked. Will you let Scripture shape your expectations in prayer? Can God's story become more fully the reference point for your story, the register against which you test the colours of your life?

Benny and Marilyn

One of the coffee-table books we have is a lavishly illustrated guide to contemporary film. Its crowning glory is a section previewing some of the best films scheduled for release in the year ahead. But the book is worse than useless when it comes to planning movie visits or DVD purchases. Why? Because it was published in 1956. *Preview 1957* is a fine piece of nostalgia (anyone for a photo-interview with Benny Hill?) and a useful historic archive (*The Best is Yet to Come*, by Marilyn Monroe).

What it cannot be is a reliable guide to the movies of 2009.

Is this how you see the Bible, as a remnant from another time, an artifact that is more interesting than useful? Only through prayer can you change such a view. Without a life of prayer, without the Holy Spirit blowing across the stirring depths of this book's oceans, you may indeed be looking at dead text. But *with* the Spirit, with the gentle beauty of a surrendered heart, with prayer – you are looking at life itself. This story tells us where we have come from, who we are and where we are going. Christian spirituality is a *storied* spirituality: it has its roots in things that have actually happened and in the stories about those things that have been passed down to us. The individual in Christian spirituality does not float in a nameless, contextless void, as if they were the first person alive. Rather, they find themselves in a story that has already started and will continue long past their part in it. *Rooted* prayer acknowledges, celebrates and is shaped by God's story through the generations of Jewish and Christian experience.

Daily fare

Andrew has discovered the power of letting Scripture shape his days and, even more, the joy of passing this habit on. Here is an e-mail he sent to us

- Several years ago, I read a testimony from a woman who said she could trace her faith back to the times as a child when she got up in the morning and found her father reading his Bible. I have often remembered this when I am reading and my daughter Rohilla comes downstairs. I sometimes wonder whether it is having any impact on her.

Now I am not trying to say I am some sort of spiritual hero here – I 'do' Quiet Time on average two or three times a week I would guess. Occasionally Rohilla has said she would like to get up and join me *in* but until now I have resisted that as I felt she was too young and that she would actually be doing it only because she thought it would make me happy. But now she is nearly 11 years old, and when she said on Sunday that she had seen a new prayer journal on the church bookstand and wanted to buy it and start doing morning Quiet Time with it, I agreed.

Monday and Tuesday we both got up together and spent half an hour reading and praying. This morning, however, my alarm failed to go off for some reason and I overslept until 07.20. I came downstairs and there was Rohilla, sitting in the chair that I usually sit in, writing in her journal. She had written a whole page about what it means to praise God.

What a fantastic moment to see her face shining. I will never forget it as long as I live. And boy do I have something to praise God for too . . .!

Scripture is life. It has fed us. It feeds us. It will feed us. It will feed our children and every generation we bring to this feast. Don't miss out on the riches set out for you in the Bible. Make them your daily fare, as vital to your health and growth as vitamins. To your rhythms of sleeping, waking, working, exercising and eating, add the rhythm of reading. In your life of prayer, whatever its pattern, weave in a thread of engagement with Scripture. Start, if you must, with a verse a day. Tear a page out, if you have to, and carry it with you until its words have found their way into your heart. Print off passages, if it helps you, and pin them to the walls and corkboards of your home and office. Find a pattern and a style that works for you to get these words and thoughts into your soul. Live your life knowing that in God's story is the hope of our planet and its people.

Exercises

Six month sentences

Some of the most inspiring words in the Bible *about* the Bible are found in Psalm 119. There are 172 verses, every one of them considering the place of God's laws and wisdom in our lives and 172 is about as close as you can get to six months at one verse each day. Take on this exercise if you really want to seek renewal in your view of Scripture. If you feel able, do it in addition to whatever other Bible reading you are doing. Here's how it works:

1. Choose a fresh, easy-to-grasp translation: the New Living Translation and Today's NIV are both good.
2. Decide how you will experience your verse-a-day. Will you write it out by hand; memorize it; text it to yourself; write out index cards? Find a way to carry the verse with you through the day.
3. Reflect through the day on this specific verse. How does this prayer strike you? Is this a metaphor you can appreciate? Are these words you would use yourself?
4. Ask God what he wants to teach you through each day's verse.

5. If you want to deepen the experience and extend its usefulness, keep a journal. Find a book (if you can) with 172 pages and jot down your impressions for each day.

At the end of this exercise, reflect on how your view of Scripture has (or hasn't!) changed. How will this impact your life of prayer?

The Google Earth view

One of the reasons we so often misread Scripture is that we fail to put each small story in the context of the one big story the Bible is telling. Having a grasp on the big story is a very important element in finding meaning in separate, smaller stories. Set aside a period of time in which you aim to get to know the Bible from a 'Google Earth View', not zooming in on verse-by-verse details but taking the wider view. Look out for resources you can use in this quest. Nick Page's book *The Big Story: What Actually Happens in the Bible*[79] is a helpful start and the CWR publication *Cover to Cover – God's Story*[80] is a deep and compelling journey through the covenants around which the Bible is built. Philip Greenslade's *A Passion for God's Story: Discovering Your Place in God's Strategic Plan*[81] will also give you a sense of God's big picture. You will have to browse these books to find out if they are accessible enough for you. Once you have found a resource that works at your level, commit to using it to get the best picture you can of the Bible's narrative: the big picture that lies under all the individual stories. Then try every time you read a specific passage to ask yourself

- Where does this fit in the big story?
- What does this passage tell me about God's plans for the world?
- How does my grasp of God's big story help me to understand and apply this passage?

Blessing

May the poems of God pursue you
And his words and letters win you
May his phrases overflow you
And his sentences surround you
May his punctuation
Purify your soul

May the legends of his love and logic
Lodge
In the cracks between intention
And fulfilment
May the vista of his sweeping story
Stretch you
To aspire to higher fires
And further freedoms

May his text complete
Your context's reconstruction
And his hope
Your habits' rehabilitation

May the words that he has spoken
That surrendered hearts have taken
Weaving into what is written
This Creator-breathed tradition
Be the path your feet are taken to
The song your soul is soaked in
May his slideshow be your gallery
May his glory
Be your story
May his memoirs
Be the making
Of your mind
Gerard Kelly

REVOLUTIONARY

Change me, change my world

> Lord, take me where You want me to go;
> Let me meet who You want me to meet;
> Tell me what You want me to say; and
> Keep me out of your way.
>
> *Father Mychal Judge*[82]

> Once having the vision, the second step to holy obedi-
> ence is this: Begin where you are. Obey now. Use what
> little obedience you are capable of, even if it be like a
> grain of mustard seed. Begin where you are.
>
> *Thomas R. Kelly*[83]

When the disciples of Jesus asked him for a lesson in
prayer, his response was to teach the words we now
know as The Lord's Prayer (Mt. 6:9–13).These are
amongst the most familiar words of the Bible and have
been translated into more languages than any other part.
This includes some exotic and unexpected languages –
but none more so than the Lord's Prayer in Klingon. As
unpronounceable as it is obscure, the official Klingon
language is something of a secret to all those outside of
the rarefied world of Star Trek but there is a language
and there is a dictionary and translation is possible. So

much so that one intrepid young 'trekkie' has chosen to go where no-one has gone before and offer a translation of the Lord's Prayer.

Every act of translation has something to teach us and most instructive here is the fact that this exercise almost failed at the seventh clause. The Klingon language has no word for forgiveness. The Klingons are a war-mongering people, a warrior-race. Their social code is built on honour and the rules of conflict. Forgiveness cannot exist, because to forgive is to admit weakness. No word has ever been created for forgiveness because no Klingon has ever felt the need to forgive. Our intrepid interpreter almost gave up, but at the last moment found a solution, by taking the concept of *revenge* – as familiar as breathing to a Klingon warrior – and putting it into its negative form so that the phrase 'forgive our sins; becomes 'you do not seek us out for revenge'. The decision *not to seek revenge* is as close as you can get as a Klingon to forgiveness.

This offers a significant insight into prayer: prayer confronts the places in our hearts and culture which have fallen out of conformity with the will of God. If God calls us to forgive and our hearts have no words for the process, then the challenge rests with us to find the words. It is God's will, not our culture, that is *normative*. This puts to death once and for all the notion that prayer is simply a projection of my personality – an extension of my dreams and desires: that I create a God in my own image and then talk to him of my ambitions. The kind of prayer Jesus is calling us to works the other way round – the more I pray, the more I am conformed to the image of God. As Tom Wright says in *The Lord and His Prayer*

> It is our birthright, as the followers of Jesus, to breathe in true divine forgiveness day by day, as the cool, clear

air which our spiritual lungs need instead of the grimy, germ-laden air that is pumped at us from all sides. And, once we start inhaling God's fresh air, there is a good chance that they will start to breathe it out, too. As we learn what it is like to be forgiven, we begin to discover that it is possible and indeed joyful, to forgive others.[84]

Transformission

The Jesus school of prayer touches on the core issues by which humanity is shaped and all too often distorted: power and dependency; greed and trust; revenge and grace. Jesus calls us to confront that within ourselves that is at odds with his purposes and to enter into a journey of change that will ultimately flow beyond ourselves. For the Klingon it is the notion of forgiveness that is too radical to consider and this is true too for many *homo sapiens*: there are more than a few whose lives have been marred by the bitterness of refusing grace: 'I don't offer mercy and I don't expect to receive it.' But there are also issues of covetousness; our inability to trust God for daily provision; of submission to God's will and direction for our lives; of courage to face and face down the evils that dominate our world. Even at the outset of the Lord's Prayer, where we are urged to come to God as our Father, some of us struggle. To be accepted; to be loved; to receive the unconditional embrace of a parent who could declare us guilty but chooses not to – this too can be a battle.

Prayer calls us to a revolution that begins with the healing of our hearts, moves outwards to the rebuilding of ruined places and calls us to move into mission: God's revolution of love reaching ultimately to the very ends of the earth. In concentric circles of grace and transformation, prayer changes me and changes my world.

Heart healing

The beginning of this revolution is in the healing of my heart. The Apostle Paul speaks for all of us when he says that 'When I want to do good, I don't. And when I try not to do wrong, I do it anyway' (Rom. 7:19, NLT). We struggle to behave as we should because, deep in our hearts, we too need healing. Transformation begins with the human heart.

The odds are against us being good, because the roots of our lack of goodness and the obstacles to us becoming good by nature are all within us. They are the weeds that have choked our better self, the barbs that render us sharp and painful to the touch. If being good came easily, surely more people would do it.

There are things *in us* that need to change before the world *around us* can. We are broken and need fixing. Skulking in the shadows just beyond our good intentions, something lurks in every human heart in need of healing. The good news, for those apprenticed to Jesus, is that prayer addresses this dilemma. There is a dimension to prayer that works inwards: that produces changes, sometimes unexpectedly, in the heart-life of the one praying. As we learn to *watch* what God is doing, one of the places we will learn to watch is within ourselves.

Jesus brought revolution to his own people, the Jews, with this different way of understanding the workings of God. *Incarnation* is more than a description of the process Jesus went through so that he could die for us: it is an expression of the deepest longing of the heart of God – to transform the world by working *from the inside* of the human heart. It is the central metaphor of the New Testament for spiritual growth. It is God's way of working. God entered into humanity in Jesus, just as surely as Jesus was formed in the humanity of Mary. In the humanity of Jesus, God dealt with the root of our rebellion and made our freedom possible. This is the freedom we are introduced to, step by step and season by season, as we grow in fruitfulness and fullness. Inner transformation – the healing of the heart – is one of the first signs we should watch for of the activity of God as we move on in the school of prayer. If we are willing and open we will always find that

> He wants to teach us that it is about his power at work in us.
> He wants to teach us that he is able to do more than we can ask or imagine.
> He wants to teach us that he is strong when we are weak.
> He wants to teach us that he is always close by and faithful in everything.
> He wants to teach us that he is a God who will never stop loving, forgiving, restarting, refreshing,
> We simply need to be willing and persevere, saying yes over and over and over again.

Knowing that God's heart for you is healing; knowing that he will not leave you in your hurts but wants to help you through; knowing that your prayers will lead to change: are you willing to stay on this journey? Will you accept his invitation to let Christ be formed in you? Can you live with an open heart, mind and soul, ready and willing for God to continually set right that which is wrong, to transform you more into this likeness, to fill your being with his life-bringing presence? Don't make the mistake of praying in words alone. Bring *intention* to the party. Surrender utterly to God and let him – in his time and his way – change you from the inside.

Ruin Rebuilding

The second area by which prayer leads us into revolution is in the call to 'rebuild ruined places.' This phrase comes from chapter 58 of the prophecies of Isaiah: powerful and poetic words that go deep to the heart of the life God asks of us.

We first met these words in the mid-1980s. We were leading the Youth for Christ team in the city of Bath and taking our earliest steps in Christian ministry. Neither of us was particularly developed either in Christian leadership or in the life of prayer, but we were driven by a passion to see God at work amongst young people and we moved nervously but joyfully from one experiment to the next. Around this time, Gerard had the unusual experience of being woken in the night – around 3am – with an overwhelming sensation that God had something important to tell him. The words that came were stark: read Isaiah 58. This was not a passage that either of us was familiar with but by morning it had been read and reread, typed out and pasted to a card that went onto our office wall and was still with us many years and many offices later.

From that moment, the words of Isaiah 58 became central to our lives and we knew that whatever work God called us to would reflect these values. We knew almost nothing about Isaiah or the context he was writing in and the words in places were strange. Surprisingly, the phrase that spoke most powerfully to us was the one we least understood

> Your people will rebuild the ancient ruins
> and will raise up the age-old foundations;
> you will be called Repairer of Broken Walls,
> Restorer of Streets with Dwellings (Is. 58:12 NIV).

To this day, we get goosebumps when we read these words: so deeply does this call resonate in us. Over twenty years we have seen time and again how a heart for prayer leads to a heart that longs for transformation. The more we know of God, the more we long to see his purposes fulfilled and the world around us healed. It is in the very nature of prayer that we will find our hearts drawn towards the 'ruined places' of our own lives and communities. As we learn to watch what God is doing, certain of the reality that God is at work *in us,* we will begin to know what it is to see God at work *through us* and the healing we have experienced as an inner reality will begin to be seen as a relational and social reality. Like a compass needle drawn towards true North, prayer works within us to pull us towards the ruined places most in need of healing. There is a directional flow in prayer *from* the quality of healing I experience in my heart *towards* the possibility of such healing in the broken places that surround me. This outward movement of transformation from a heart experience to a changed world is the essential dance that stops prayer from becoming a me-fest. Even if I want to pray always and only about my own needs, I find I cannot, because genuine prayer – genuine openness to God – draws my heart to ruined places.

The softening of our heart in prayer prepares soil for the seeds of obedience to grow in; our exposure to the compassionate Christ stirs in us compassion. That which begins in the heart renews the mind and finds expression through the hands. Here is Dave Westlake's account of discovering the boundaries of this reality in India:

I was on a trip to India with Tearfund once, visiting people we work with in Bombay. I had a day off in the middle and was taken by a friend to a place called the Gate of India, in the city's bay. There's an expensive hotel there called the Taj as well as plenty of street entertainers, snake charmers, stalls and the like. It's a fun place to be and it's awash with tourists. It's also full of children who are begging. Having got wise to the way of the world, whenever they see a Western person they tend to bombard them with requests for cash. My friend advised me not to give them anything as once you started it wouldn't take long before a crowd of forty children might be chasing you. The whole thing could get a little scary and it was best left alone. Having looked around we got into a taxi and headed off to our next destination.

The cab stopped at some traffic lights right outside the Taj Hotel and, as usual, while we waited people approached the open windows to try and sell us goods or to beg. One girl walked up, and looked at me. 'Please, Uncle,' she said. Uncle is a term of respect in India, used in much the same way as we would say 'sir.' I looked at the girl and saw that she was around ten or twelve, was very beautiful and dressed in a piece of cloth. Again she asked for money, 'Please, Uncle.'

The traffic lights changed and we moved on before I had the chance to get any money out. I turned to my friend and said how beautiful she was. 'Yes,' he replied, 'she was, wasn't she? It's a shame, as within a year or two she'll probably be a prostitute and then she'll be lucky to make it into her twenties.'

It was later on that night as I was thinking about my day that I realised I knew who that little girl was. Her name was Jesus. One day I'll stand in front of him and hear the words coming at me: 'I was hungry and you did not feed me. I was thirsty and you did not give me a drink. I was a stranger and you did not invite me in, naked and you did not clothe me.'

And I'll say, 'But when didn't I do these things?'

He'll say, 'You were in a taxi in Bombay, waiting for the traffic lights outside the Taj Hotel to change. For as much as you did not do it for the least of these, my brothers and sisters, you did not do it for me.'[85]

Isaiah 58 calls for us, in essence, to do two things if we want to join God's world rebuilding programme. The first is to care for the poor in our midst. The prophet mentions ending conflict, freeing those wrongly imprisoned; treating workers fairly; feeding the hungry; welcoming strangers; giving clothes to those who need them; helping those in every kind of need. His list overlaps conspicuously with that used by Jesus in Matthew 25, urging compassion for the hungry, the thirsty, strangers, the naked, the sick and those in prison. Jesus would have known the Isaiah passage well and his own thinking was doubtless deeply shaped by it. But in all this emphasis on *actions* that display compassion, Isaiah makes a second claim upon our time. He asks us to honour God's institution of the Sabbath.

Keep the Sabbath day holy. Don't pursue your own interests on that day, but enjoy the Sabbath and speak of it with delight as the LORD's holy day. Honour the LORD in everything you do, and don't follow your own desires or talk idly. If you do this, the Lord will be your delight. I will give you great honour and give you your full share of the inheritance I promised to Jacob, your ancestor. I, the LORD, have spoken! (Is. 58:13-14, NLT)

This unexpected shift from compassionate action to Sabbath rest has many layers of meaning, not least of which is its overtone of justice – with regulations about letting workers rest, leaving land fallow, cancelling debts and freeing slaves. Sabbath principles speak directly to issues of economic justice-keeping. But they also speak, as we have earlier explored, of rest and rhythm, of the intentional creation of God-ward spaces in our calendars.

Isaiah is telling us that we become rebuilders in a broken world through a weaving together of two threads: merciful action and deep Sabbath rest. Contemplation and action; prayer and service; inward peace and outward love; silence before the Almighty and a loud shout for the poor – these are not opposites that demand we make a choice: they are the polarities by which our life with God is forged. We shouldn't be afraid to step back from action to seek rest in the presence of God and we shouldn't be surprised when, out of rest, we are compelled into transformative action. We sense this movement beginning when *even in our prayers* we begin to feel with God the agony of unhealed hurt in the world beyond our doors. The most impacting journey into action is the journey that has already begun before we even rise from prayer.

The bridge between the inner life of prayer and the outer world of action is the word *compassion*, because compassion is both feeling and action. In its deepest sense compassion means 'to share the sufferings of'. The person on whom I have compassion is the person *whose sufferings become mine* and this is a journey that begins in my soul but moves in due course to my muscles. I share the suffering in the travail of my own heart and I share the suffering by taking part of the burden. I am *moved with compassion* to see you carrying more shopping bags than are good for you and I *move with compassion* by taking two bags from you. Like a rope tying a boat to the quayside, compassion stretches from my heart to your need. It is anchored in the feelings God stirs in my heart, but is thrown outwards in the tasks God entrusts to my hands. Prayer is vital because the rebuilding begins in my heart. Action is vital because it doesn't stop there. John Stott suggests that this pattern of heart to hand is the very essence of the ministry of Jesus

> Jesus was not afraid to look human need in the face, in all its ugly reality. And what he saw invariably moved him to compassion and so to passionate service. Sometimes, he spoke. But his compassion never dissipated itself in words; it found expression in deeds. He saw, he felt, he acted. The movement was from the eye to the heart, and from the heart to the hand. His compassion was always aroused by the sight of need, and it always led to constructive action.[86]

As we grow in the Jesus school of prayer we can expect our praying hearts to be drawn from self obsession to awareness of our broken world. The deeper we go, the further our dreams will carry. We can ask God to open our eyes to the ruined places that surround us; we can bring what we see into the place of prayer and let it cook until we find our hands and feet compelled to go to where our hearts have gone already.

We forge our commitment to action in the place of Sabbath rest because that which God does in us by his Spirit is *of the same substance* as that which he does in his world. Hebrews 7:22 describes Jesus as 'the guarantee of a better covenant' and three times, in 2 Corinthians 1:22, 2 Corinthians 5:5 and Ephesians 1:14, Paul describes the Holy Spirit as a 'deposit' guaranteeing God's future promises to us. The presence of the

Spirit in our lives guarantees our inheritance – he is a part-payment proving that what is to come will come – but he also allows us to *taste* our inheritance. His actions in us now show us what the healing of the world will look like.

Revolutionary prayer takes hold of the passions and emotions of the heart and puts them to good use in our spiritual journey: it is prayer that accepts and carries the dangerous reality of an emotional charge. It is a call to pour out the perfume of my worship in the place of prayer and the perfume of my actions for the poor; to let my prayers rise up as incense before the throne of God (Rev. 5:8; Rev. 8:3–4) and let my life have the sweet-smelling fragrance of being good news in the world (2 Cor. 2:14–15). Instead of picturing this as a prayer with both hands lifted to Heaven, try seeing it as a prayer in which, with one hand, we reach up to take the hand of our Father and, with the other, reach out into our world, to grasp the hands of those in need. That way we will connect with the certainty of his purposes and rest in the vastness of his capacity to love us, while also identifying with those for whom the promise of redemption remains a future hope, standing with those who suffer. And in between the two – a hand to Heaven and a hand to earth – we say 'I won't let go.' This is the true meaning of prayer, to wrestle as Jacob did with the twin realities that face us; the awe-inspiring promises of Heaven and the terrifying pains of earth and to say 'I won't let go.'

This was the kind of wrestling that seemed to be weighing heavy on the mind of rock star Bono when he received the 2007 'Chairman's Award' from the NAACP – The National Association for the Advancement of Coloured Peoples. In a speech that found its way within minutes around the blogosphere, Bono spoke for the frustrations of longings of many when he placed faith at the very centre of human need

> This is true religion. True religion will not let us fall asleep in the comfort of our freedom. 'Love thy neighbour' is not a piece of advice, it's a command. And that means that in the global village we're going to have to start loving a whole lot more people. Where you live should not decide whether you live or whether you die. And to those in the church who still sit in judgement on the aids emergency, let me climb into the pulpit for just one moment, because whatever thoughts we have about God; who he is or even if God exists, most will agree that God has a special place for the poor. The poor are where God lives. God is in the slums, in the cardboard boxes where the poor play house. God is where the opportunity is lost and lives are shattered. God is with the mother who has infected her child with a virus that will take both their lives. God is under the rubble in the cries we hear during war time. God, my friends, is with the poor, and God is with us if we are with them.

Is this the kind of passion that stirs in your heart every time you come to prayer? Is your Jesus a compliant Christ who benevolently blesses your dry and unengaged religion – or a prophet who rattles your cage? What fires is God trying to light, through prayer, in your heart?

Mission moving

The third way in which prayer invites me to a revolution is that it urges me to *move into mission*, embracing the planet-wide scope of the purposes of God. A phrase often used in management thinking is to *begin with the end in mind*. Business leaders are urged to envision the ultimate goal of the work they are engaged in and to make decisions now informed by the future. This is not as radical as some might think. Ploughmen have understood for centuries that the best way to plough straight is to find a fixed point on the edge of the field and look steadfastly towards it. Looking at the blade of the plough just leads to trouble. Seamstresses use the same technique to cut cloth. The hand is on the scissors, but the eye is fixed on the point towards which the scissors are moving. Keep your hand on the task but your eye on the horizon. This may well have been the thought that Jesus had in mind when he warned that 'Anyone who puts a hand to the plough and then looks back is not fit for the Kingdom of God.' (Lk. 9:62, NLT). Perhaps he knew what his mostly agricultural audience were thinking – that the worker in question wasn't fit to be much of a ploughman either. Never mind the Kingdom, I wouldn't even want him on my farm.

This principle holds true as much for praying as for ploughing. Our prayers will focus on real and immediate needs – the blade of plough or scissors must cut into actual soil and actual cloth and prayer achieves little unless it cuts into real needs in real times and real places. But our prayers will be shaped and directed and given fresh imaginative power if they are prayed with one eye to the horizon. And on the horizon, in God's end-game, the landscape is very different from the one you saw when you opened your curtains this morning.

God's story is a project that, more than any other, has begun with the end in mind. From covenant promises delivered to Adam, Noah and Abraham; through a patchwork of prophetic dreams released over the centuries; to the promises of Jesus and the cinematic climax of John's revelation – God has let us in on his plans. The question 'Where is this all going?' does not remain unanswered long for the student of the Jesus school of prayer

> The Bible has a captivating view of the goal or climax of mission. It describes a future in which every language, people group and country will be represented altogether in a magnificent display of international co-operation and harmony (Revelation 7:9).The whole of history is moving towards this stupendous conclusion: a planet-wide worship and celebration event drawn from all the nations of the globe under the Lordship of Jesus.[87]

God does not seem to want us to know the details or timetable of his plans – even Jesus spoke of these as hidden things[88] – but he does want us to have a sense of how our journey ends, a flavour of the goal towards which we are praying. The horizon in the light of which we pray is defined not only by the vastness of God and of his love for us, but also by his self-revealed determination to bless our world. Just as sky and earth meet at the horizon, so our future lies in the union of earth and Heaven, where the love of God and the plans of God come together. We are on a collision course with the blessing of God: there's a party at the end of our tunnel. This is significant to our life of prayer because

- There is an intimate connection between prayer and mission: we meet the person of God in our praying and are drawn into the purposes of God in our world.
- The ultimate horizon of our prayers, therefore, is the horizon of God's mission: the earth freed, the creation blessed, every tribe and tongue and nation healed.

- Prayer is a doorway into the mission of God in the world. To step through this door is to embrace the global nature of prayer.
- As prayer *connects us to* and *draws us into* God's global intentions, there is no limit to how far we can travel.

Be the love revolution

To pray is to step into a revolution whose ultimate scope is cosmic. The Holy Spirit invites us to play opposite him in a great unfolding drama that began before we even entered the theatre and will in all likelihood continue past our leaving. This is a lifetime's adventure. Our God is producing a *kingdom*, a global empire of obedience in which every language has its lines to speak and every people group its part. If prayer has lost its passion in many of our churches, it may well be because mission has lost its meaning for us.

One of the greatest joys we experience in leading short-term mission teams for the Bless Network has been in seeing this connection restored. By centring our mission trips on prayer and challenging participants to pepper their prayers with passion for mission, we have seen a reawakening in both domains: young leaders more energized than they have ever been in prayer and more willing than they ever thought they could be to engage in mission. Reconnect with the purposes of God: let prayer inspire your love of mission and mission ignite your love for prayer. Prayer places you at the centre of God's purposes in the world and no matter how small you believe yourself to be, your dialogue is with the limitless scope of the purposes of God.

Prayer and the *missio dei*

If mission is to shape and stretch our prayers, it is important that it be God's mission, not ours. Theologians use the Latin term *missio dei* to catch the concept of God's mission in the world. The God to whom we pray is the God who has initiated mission in the world. He sets its course. He defines its scope. Its shape reflects his character. His glory is its goal – the ultimate end of mission is that God will be worshipped. The more we hear his heart in prayer the better we will understand his plan. The more we see the breadth of his plan, the more we will be driven to discover him in prayer. We do not pray for the success of our projects, for the prosperity of our churches, for the meeting of our missional goals. We pray for the glory of God. We follow the Spirit into mission and cheer him on. 'Mission is ultimately God's', Andrew Lord writes, 'and we cannot determine how the Spirit may work, but rather we need to follow the Spirit's lead in the hope of the change our God can and will bring.'[89]

Prayer as virtual travelling

The whole world is included in the scope of God's love. The whole world is burdened in some way with need. No passport is needed to tour the world in prayer. No carbon emissions are involved. No tedious check-in queues and security routines will spoil the journey. Choose your destination. Take off now. Prayer is the world's most accessible form of transport and, like the earth seen from space, it knows no borders. To bring your prayer to mission and mission to your prayer is to become a *world* Christian, a believer who has understood that kingdom is primary and culture secondary. And this realization is born in prayer.

The many cultures of the world are like faces on a beautifully cut diamond. Each reflects a different facet of the glory of God. The Creator has left pieces of his jigsaw all around for us to hunt for. Finding them, putting them together, seeing the picture emerge is a source of incomparable joy.

What greater adventure could we enjoy than to see God's Kingdom emerge in all the places on our planet he is working? And perhaps the greatest joy is the discovery that the scope of the Creator's plans is not limited even to the breadth of the human race. Vast and diverse as it may be, even the full span of humanity is not enough to exhaust God's love. His mission extends into the deepest core of the universe: the very atoms of matter will be redeemed. Commenting on Romans 8:18–21, Philip Greenslade and Selwyn Hughes suggest that

> In his stunning prophetic vision, Paul sees the destiny of believers and the future of creation mysteriously intertwined. As we know, our sin dragged creation down into fallenness and frustration. Now, strangely, our redemption offers hope to a groaning world . . . Hear with wonder the promise that the power released through the new creation will one day affect the old creation. The last word in the universe will not be a groan but Joy! Joy! Joy![90]

Is this not the best of news? Is this not a goal worth praying for, a travail worth sharing? Our universe is scheduled for redemption: will we not, with joy, embrace the company of its Redeemer?

Land here

In our work with the Bless Network we have discovered that we can move beyond prayer *for* mission to engage in prayer *as* mission. By moving into the places where mission is happening, we can stand alongside local believers and add our prayers to their efforts to celebrate and demonstrate God's Kingdom. We have been inspired over the years to devote more and more of our 'missional' timetable to prayer and we have stopped believing that prayer is only useful if it flows into some specific missional activity. Prayer is useful because it calls into being the rule of God. We stand on ground we may not own and say, as far as we are able on behalf of God's confused and captive creatures, 'Heaven here, Heaven now. Let the empire of your love arrive.' Like villagers lining up with torches to show the bush pilot where to land, we cry to God – 'Land here!' And where we are not local, we can stand with those who are, adding our faith to theirs and perhaps encouraging their efforts. We have grown increasingly to understand that prayer is not merely an accompaniment to God's purposes – the French fries to the burger of God's business, the mayo on the side of mission. In senses so deep we are only beginning to discover them, prayer *is* mission. When we pray, we are not accessorizing mission. We are engaging in it. Pray without ceasing, Paul says, because the battle we are called to is not waged with human weapons.

The other side

Perhaps our need, if we are to embrace the connection of mission to prayer, is to learn the lessons Peter learned in his brief years with Jesus. 'Let down your nets on the other side' the Master called out to him, for only then will you see the sheer extravagance of God's plans for his creation. Without these lessons and those that followed later, when dreams and visions and the voice of the Spirit showed Peter just how far 'the other side' might be, might he have held on to a smaller view of God? Might he have believed in a domesticated Jesus, reaching the Jews and a few chosen Gentiles who happened to be lurking at their fringes? Might Peter have been content to think small if Jesus and the Holy Spirit hadn't challenged him? Had that been so, many things would be different in the world. We, to name just two, would not know Christ. And neither, we suspect, would you. Is your God too small, too local, too limited to your familiar pathways? Is the life of prayer he calls you to a life of expanding vision, of limitless scope, of global goals and planetary perspectives? Is it time for you to let your nets down on the other side?

Reflection: Let down your nets

Let down your nets
On the other side
Peter
On the other side of your fears
On the other side of doubt
On the other side of your certainties
On the other side
Of who you think you are

On the other side of staying in the boat
Step out onto the waves towards me
On the other side of panic
Reach out your hand to mine
On the other side of your reputation, Simon
Become Peter, the movable rock
On the other side of haste

Of your hot head
Of violence
Put away your sword
On the other side of the lake
On the other side of town
Follow me to the other side of the tracks
Explore the other side of life

Seek the sheep
On the other side of the mountain
See the other side of the coin
Find the other side of the father
In the other side of his lost son
On the other side of religion
The other side of law
On the other side of the temple
The other side of the wall
On the other side of obedience
The other side of love
On the other side of forgiveness
Hear the seventy-times-seven
Other sides of the story

Though tears will fall
On the other side of the sunrise
You will laugh
On the other side of your face
On the other side of this side of Heaven

On the other side of denial
On the other side of loss
On the other side of Pentecost
Let down your nets . . .

Exercises

Inner Change Audit

Create space and make time to answer a few questions about your own spiritual formation. Think over your life of prayer of the past twelve months and ask yourself

Where have your struggles been?

What are the main factors that seem to stunt your growth or slow down the process of Christ being formed in you? Don't think for the moment about what you might do about any of these, just make a note in single words or short phrases of the things that come to mind.

Are you trying too hard?

Are there areas in which you can see a pattern of trying and failing, trying and failing? How can you shift to being *teachable* in these areas? Set aside time for each of these areas to renew your prayers in three stages:

Repent of being better at trying than at asking for help

Rely on God. Ask him to direct your thoughts and actions and to lead you in this area.

Respond to God by committing to a new course of action from his word to you.

Have you been disengaged?

Do you retreat for periods because of guilt or lack of focus or just spiritual laziness? Ask God to show you if there were times when he came knocking at your door and you wouldn't let him in? When did you *escape* instead of *praying*?

Can you set 'formation goals' for the coming year?

Are there areas where your prayer could be bolder or your aspirations higher? Are you ready to be stretched in your vision for your spiritual life? Ask God to show you key areas in which objectives could be set. What changes do you long to see? As you pray through these, about which do you sense a prompting of the Spirit that this issue is 'for such a time as this'?

OCD redeemed

Is there a particular nation, region or people group God has put on your heart for prayer? If so, how obsessive are you about learning more? Is your home filled with maps and books about them? Do you take every opportunity to learn more? Have you ever been to your nearest library and said 'Give me everything you've got on . . .?' The dividing line between passion and OCD can be quite thin. Sometimes it is not wrong to be a little obsessed! Investing time and energy to explore a particular prayer burden has a double impact. If this really is a call from God to pray, you will find that the more you know, the more you want to pray. Added information will only increase the obsession. If it is not a long-term God-given call, you will find that an overdose of information puts you off but at least you will know where your heart is. Don't start with a recent interest – examine your own heart to ask 'What is there that has stirred my heart from the very start?' Make this the area you commit to exploring more.

The Other Side

Set aside some quiet time and space and take two large sheets of paper (flip chart paper is ideal) and some felt-tip pens. On one piece of paper write **My Side** and list there the people, places and situations that are regularly part of your life. These might be regular subjects of prayer for you. Take a few moments to pray God's blessing on these people, just as you may well have done before. Now take the second piece of paper and head it **The Other Side**. Ask God to help you and begin to list people, places and situation that come to mind – i.e. you know about them – but have never been subjects of your prayers. Review your '**Other Side**' sheet and ask yourself three questions

> Are there people, places or situations here that God is challenging me to pray for more frequently?
>
> If so, what will that require of me? Do I need more information? Should I ask what their needs are? How do I decide what to pray for?
>
> Am I prepared to do it?

Word swap

Paul Marshall suggests that we should be aware

> Just how much of the Bible is about justice. The word 'righteousness', which we often use instead, seems to have different connotations in the modern world and is often used by Christians to mean 'holiness' or 'morality.' However, if we substitute, as we should, variations of the term 'justice' wherever we read 'righteousness', then the Bible begins to sound quite different We realise that justice appears and is stressed again and again through-out the Scriptures in reference to God, to Jesus Christ, to kings, judges, priests, prophets, the poor and the rich.[91]

Try taking this plea seriously. As you read Scripture, whenever you come across the word 'righteousness' or concepts such as 'right living', substitute 'justice' instead. How does this affect your reading? How might it impact what you pray for and how you pray?

God's words, your words

Read these words of Jesus from Luke 4, based on Isaiah 61

> The Spirit of the Lord is upon me, for he has appointed me to preach Good News to the poor. He has sent me to proclaim that captives will be released, that the blind will see, that the downtrodden will be freed from their oppressors, and that the time of the Lord's favour has come (Lk. 4:18-19, NLT).

Now imagine them as your words. You are giving this speech at *your* local church. How do you feel as you speak these words? What would your friends and family think? As you speak each phrase, what images come to mind? Are there people and situations you find yourself thinking about? How might the answers to these questions change your prayers?

Start in the heart

Review the last three or six months of your life. Try to remember three times that your heart was stirred with compassion. What were the circumstances? Whose needs were you moved by? Did you make those needs the subject of ongoing prayer? If not, what would you need to do so – more information? More determination? Ask God to show you in the coming 24 hours some specific needs he wants you to carry in prayer. Commit to it and find creative ways to do it.

Step over the threshold

As an exercise in transforming prayer, find time to prayer-walk your own neighbourhood. Ask God to open your eyes as you walk, to the needs he wants you to take on: first in prayer and maybe then in action.

Secret pastor

Ask God if he is calling you, in prayer, to become the secret pastor of your street: praying for your neighbours and their needs exactly as you would if you were in a prayer group together. Ask yourself: how should I find what to pray for? How do I know when my prayers are answered? Watch out for God-given opportunities to know your neighbours better, to bless them through action as well as prayer, to refine and deepen your prayers for them.

City Changing Prayer

Reflect on whether there are key issues for the transforming of your city that you can pray about with others. Read *City Changing Prayer* by Frank and Debra Green[92] – the story of the Manchester prayer network. Could this happen in your village, town, school or office? Could you be one of the initiators?

Prayer, Art, Justice

Read one of the books that tells the story of the 24/7 prayer movement. Try *Red Moon Rising*,[93] *The Vision and the Vow*[94] or *Punk Monk*.[95] What do you learn about the connection between prayer and justice? How can you give arms and legs to this connection?

The Holy Spirit's mission

One of the twentieth century pioneers of a charismatic approach to the Christian life was the late John Wimber, founder of the Vineyard movement. From the publication of his first book *Power Evangelism* onwards, Wimber introduced many Christians to the added dimension brought to faith, life, worship and mission by the dynamic experience of God's Spirit.

And it all began with three small words. For Wimber and those who followed his lead, three simple words of invitation to the third person of the Trinity changed everything: 'Come Holy Spirit' . . .

So let's take a moment to pray these vital words and reflect on the areas of our own lives and vision that the coming of the Holy Spirit might revolutionize . . .

Prayer

Come Holy Spirit
Pause

In the places where we are dry and broken and have lost
the joy of God . . .
Come Holy Spirit
pause

Where we face obstacles and challenges
that are too much for us.
Where our strength is simply not enough to get us
through . . .
Come Holy Spirit
pause

Where those we know and love are struggling.
Where friends and family need to know God's love;
to receive his grace; to be transformed by his power . . .
Come Holy Spirit
pause

Where our cities struggle with the burden of too much
sin;
too many questions;
too many false answers.
Where our nations flounder for the loss of their faith . . .
Come Holy Spirit
pause

Come Holy Spirit to our families.
Come Holy Spirit to our neighbourhoods and towns.
Come Holy Spirit to our church.
To our homes and hearts: Come Holy Spirit.

Blessing: Everything we bring

This blessing was written for a time of Communion. Use it in that setting or set out bread and wine just for yourself. Let these symbols represent your life of prayer. Hold them in your heart as an image of your intimacy with God and let these words speak of the whole footprint of that relationship in your life.

Everything we bring

Everything we bring
To this place
Finds a place here
Every case that we carry can be consigned here
Every load we are lifting can be left
Every secret we are slaves to can be spoken here
Every terror that torments us can be told.

There is room here for anguish
For the agony of abandonment
There is ground here for grieving
For the weeping wounds of loss
In this circle of safety
At this fireside of faith
There is space for story and song
There is room for revelation and renewal
Here is hope and healing
Here is forgiveness and freedom
Here is connection and correction
And coming to our senses

At this source
Whose depths are never ending

This river
That will never run dry
At this table
Whose banquet of abundance
Knows no bounds

No wrong
Is too wrong
To be righted here
No tragedy too twisted
To be turned
For everything we bring
To this place
Finds a place here
And every load we are lifting can be left

Gerard Kelly

Blessing: Love me Into Love

Love me into loving
Jesus
Grow me
Into grace
Set me up
For servanthood
Forge
Forgiveness in me
Pour me out in passion
Mould me into mercy
Caress me into caring

Lord
Recreate me
To the core

As your worship
To the Father
As your love-gift
To the world
As your act
Of crafted kindness
As the music
Of your soul

Break the seals
Tip the bottle
Squeeze
The perfume out
Turn me towards tenderness
Lord
Love me into Love

Gerard Kelly

Endnotes

[1] Matthew 11:25–30 *The Message*: italics mine.

[2] John 5:19 'I assure you, the Son can do nothing by himself. He does only what he sees the Father doing. Whatever the Father does, the Son also does.'

[3] See Kelly, G., *Retrofuture* (Downers Grove: IVP, 2000) for a description of our post-industrial, post-literate, post-modern, post-imperial and post-Christian future.

[4] Hybels, B., *Too Busy Not to Pray* (Downers Grove: IVP, 1998).

[5] Williams, R., BBC Radio Two, October 18th 2006, cited in *The Times*, London, October 19th 2006.

[6] Wright, T., *Surprised by Hope* (London: SPCK, 2007), p291.

[7] Christine Sine, *Sacred Rhythms: Finding a Peaceful Pace in a Hectic World* (Grand Rapids: Baker Books, 2003).

[8] Wilson-Hartgrove in a forthcoming book, *New Monasticism: What It Has to Say to Today's Church*, cited in 'The Unexpected Monks' in *The Boston Globe*, by Molly Worthen, Feb 3rd 2008, accessed at http://www.boston.com/bostonglobe/ideas/articles/2008/02/03/the_unexpected_monks/?page=2 accessed Sept 3rd 2008.

[9] Cited in Ball, P., *Bright Earth – The Invention of Colour* (London: Vintage Books, 2008), p200.

[10] Ball, P., *Bright Earth – The Invention of Colour* (London: Vintage Books, 2008), p200.

[11] The Liturgy of Abundance, The Myth of Scarcity by Walter Brueggemann. This article appeared in the *Christian Century*, March 24–31, 1999. Cited at Religion Online http://www.religion-online.org/showarticle.asp?title=533 accessed September 3rd 2008.

[12] Macdonald, G., *Ordering Your Private World* (Nashville: Thomas Nelson, 1984).

[13] 'Rhythms of Life' Posted on September 15, 2007 by Christine Sine at http://godspace.wordpress.com/2007/09/15/rhythms-of-life/ accessed September 3rd 2008.

[14] *'What is a Spiritual Practice*?' Posted on July 9, 2008 by Christine Sine at http://godspace.wordpress.com/2008/07/09/what-is-a-spiritual-practice/ accessed September 3rd 2008.

[15] Hayford, J., *Worship His Majesty: How Praising the King of Kings Will Change Your Life* (Ventura: Gospel Light Productions, 2000).

[16] Cited in J. Robertson, *Windows to Eternity* (Abingdon: Bible Reading Fellowship, 1999).

[17] Kelly, G., *Spoken Worship* (Grand Rapids: Zondervan, 2007).

[18] 'Rhythms of Life' Posted on September 15, 2007 by Christine Sine at http://godspace.wordpress.com/2007/09/15 /rhythms-of-life/ accessed September 3rd 2008.

[19] De Caussade, J-P., *The Sacrament of the Present Moment*, translated by Kitty Muggeridge from the original text of the treatise on *Self-Abandonment to Divine Providence* (London: Fount Paperbacks, 1981)

[20] Fernando, A., *Missionaries for the right reasons*, talk given at the annual conference of the Evangelical Missionary Alliance, 1997, accessed at http://www.urbana.org/_articles.cfm?RecordId=133 accessed Setpoember 5th 2008.

[21] Freeman, A., *'The 24-7Boiler Room Rule: The Purposes, Principles, Practices and Customary Requisite of a Licensed 24-7 Boiler Room Community'*, Paper submitted to the 24/7 Round Table, Herrnhut, Germany, September 2005.

22 Meister Eckhart (c. 1260–1327) German Christian mystic, from '*Journey in Word*,' ed. Cyndi Craven; an Internet collection of quotations, http://www.spiritsong.com/quotes / accessed September 8th 2008.

23 '*To Pray Without Ceasing*', Posted on November 27, 2007 by Christine Sine at http://godspace.wordpress.com /2007/11/27/to-pray-without-ceasing/ Accessed September 8th 2008.

24 www.WatershedCharlotte.com.

25 Cited in Mitton, M., *Restoring the Woven Cord* (London: Darton, Longman & Todd Ltd, 1995).

26 Peterson, E.,A *Long Obedience in the Same Direction* (Downers Grove: IVP, 2000).

27 Rosenblatt, R., (June 14, 1999). 'TIME 100: Heroes & Icons of the 20th century, Anne Frank', *Time* magazine. http://www.time.com/time/time100/heroes/profile/fra nk01.html accessed September 12th 2008.

28 Rosenblatt, R., (June 14, 1999). 'TIME 100: Heroes & Icons of the 20th century, Anne Frank', *Time* magazine. http://www.time.com/time/time100/heroes/profile /frank01.html accessed September 12th 2008.

29 *Anne Frank's Diary*, Pan Books, 1968, cited in Rolheiser, R., *Forgotten Among the Lilies: Learning to Love Beyond our Fears* (New York: Doubleday, 2005).

30 Rolheiser, R., *Forgotten Among the Lilies: Learning to Love Beyond our Fears* (New York: Doubleday, 2005).

31 Rolheiser, R., *Forgotten Among the Lilies: Learning to Love Beyond our Fears* (New York: Doubleday, 2005).

32 Rolheiser, R., *Forgotten Among the Lilies: Learning to Love Beyond our Fears* (New York: Doubleday, 2005).

33 Meister Eckhart cited in Yancey, P., *Reaching for the Invisible God: What Can We Expect to Find*? (Grand Rapids: Zondervan 2004).

34 Based on the multiple references Jesus makes to the life of Daniel, including his use of the term 'Son of Man', it is

clear that he was both familiar with and influenced by Daniel's story.

35 Lucas, E., *Apollos Old Testament Commentary: Daniel* (Leicester: IVP, 2002).

36 Brueggemann, W., *Finally comes the Poet: Daring Speech for Proclamation* (Minneapolis: Augsburg Fortress Press, 1989).

37 Fernando, A., *Spiritual Living in a Secular World* (Oxford: Monarch, 2002).

38 Ravenhill, L., *Why Revival Tarries* (Grand Rapids: Bethany House, 1979).

39 Davidson, D & D, with George Verwer, *God's Great Ambition* (Carlisle: Authentic, 2001).

40 Ignatius of Antioch, attributed.

41 Webber, R., *Ancient-Future Faith* (Grand Rapids: Baker books, 2000).

42 Fretheim, T. E., *Interpretation: Exodus* (Louisville: John Knox, 1991).

43 Fretheim, T. E., *Interpretation: Exodus*, p315 (Louisville: John Knox, 1991).

44 Robertson, J., *Windows to Eternity* (Abingdon: Bible Reading Fellowship, 1999).

45 Expositors Bible Commentary, CD Rom (Grand Rapids: Zondervan, 2006).

46 Fretheim, T. E., *Interpretation: Exodus* (Louisville: John Knox, 1991).

47 Fretheim, T. E., *Interpretation: Exodus* (Louisville: John Knox, 1991).

48 Noble, J., *The Shaking* (Oxford: Monarch, 2002).

49 Morgan, A., *Learning to Pray*, Internet article posted at http://alisonmorgan.co.uk/Learning%20to%20pray.htm accessed September 12th 2008.

50 Piper, J., *Desiring God* (Leicester: IVP, 1994).

51 A phrase coined by poet Stewart Henderson.

52 Noble, J., *The Shaking* (Oxford: Monarch, 2002).

53 Robertson, J., *Windows to Eternity*, p57 (Abingdon: Bible Reading Fellowship, 1999).

54 Bosch, D., *Transforming Mission* (Maryknoll, NY: Orbis Books, 1992).

55 Draper, B. & K., *Refreshing Worship* (Abingdon: Bible Reading Fellowship, 2000).

56 Walker, A., *Telling the Story* (London: SPCK, 1996).

57 Amy Roche is a church planter in Perpignan, France and works with the Bless Network. Unpublished material c. the author.

58 Muir, B., and R. Crowne, *The Art of Connecting* (Carlisle: Authentic, 2003).

59 Hector Gimenez's testimony, *The Miraculous Power of God*, can be obtained from Kingdom Faith Ministries (www.kingdomfaith.com). Cited by Alison Morgan, Changing Individuals: living in the Truth of Christ, Fulcrum http://www.fulcrum-anglican.org.uk/page .cfm?ID=273.

60 Andrew Hawkins, Canadian author of *Whispers That Delight: Building a Listening-Centered Prayer Life* comments accessed at http://listeningprayer.net/.

61 Carretto, C., *Letters from the Desert*, translated by Rose Mary Hancock (London: Darton, Longman and Todd, 1972).

62 *Phoebe Palmer*, *Selected Writings*, ed. Oden, T.C., Paulist Press, 1988 cited in Foster, R., *Streams of Living Water* (San Francisco: Harper San Francisco, 2001).

63 Brueggemann, W., *Biblical Perspectives on Evangelism* (Nashville: Abingdon Press, 1993).

64 Gaukroger, S., *Why Bother with Mission?* p132 (Leicester: IVP, 1996).

65 Borst, J., *Coming to God in the Stillness* (Stowmarket: Kevin Mayhew, 2008).

66 Evelyn Underhill cited in Richard J. Foster & Emilie Griffin, Spiritual Classics: Selected Readings for Individuals and Groups on the Twelve Spiritual *Disciplines* (New York: HarperCollins, 2000).

[67] Beckett, F., *Called To Action* (Grand Rapids: Zondervan, 1989.

[68] Price, P., cited in *Mission Shaped Church* (London: Church House Publishing, 2004).

[69] Dietrich Bonhoeffer *Life Together* (Norwich: SCM, 1954).

[70] Cited in Robertson, J., *Windows on Eternity* (Abingdon: Bible Reading Fellowship, 1999).

[71] Wurmbrand, R., *Tortured For Christ* (Bartlesville: Living Sacrifice Book Company, 1967).

[72] Peterson, E., *Eat This Book* (Grand Rapids: Eerdmans, 2006).

[73] Foster, R., and Kathryn A Helmers, *Life with God* (London: Hodder and Stoughton, 2008).

[74] Foster, R., and Kathryn A. Helmers, *Life with God* (London: Hodder and Stoughton, 2008).

[75] Tidball, D., *The Message of the Cross* (Leicester: IVP, 2001).

[76] Boyd, G., *God at War* (Leicester: IVP, 1997).

[77] Amy Roche is a church planter in Perpignan, France and works with the Bless Network. Unpublished material c. the author.

[78] Daniel 3:17–18, *The Street Bible* (Grand Rapids: Zondervan, 2002).

[79] Page, N., *The Big Story* (Milton Keynes: Spring Harvest publishing division/Authentic Lifestyle, 2007).

[80] Greenslade, P., *Cover to Cover: God's Story* (Farnham: CWR, 2001).

[81] Greenslade, P., *A Passion for God's Story* (Milton Keynes: Paternoster, 2002).

[82] Father Mychal Judge was a Roman Catholic Chaplain of the New York Fire Department. He died in the course of his duties on September 11th 2001. Cited at http://saintmychaljudge.blogspot.com/ accessed September 18th 2008.

[83] Kelly, T.R., *Holy Obedience*, William Penn Lecture 1939, Delivered at Arch Street Meeting House Philadelphia, cited at http://www.quaker.org/pamphlets/wpl1939a.html accessed November 1st 2008.

84 Wright, T., *The Lord and His Prayer* (Grand Rapids, Eerdmans 1997).

85 Westlake, D., *Upwardly Mobile* (London: Hodder and Stoughton, 2001).

86 Cited in Gaukroger, S., *Why Bother With Mission?* (Leicester: IVP, 1996).

87 Gaukroger, S., *Why Bother With Mission?* (Leicester: IVP, 1996).

88 Acts 1:6-8 'When the apostles were with Jesus, they kept asking him, 'Lord, are you going to free Israel now and restore our kingdom?' 'The Father sets those dates,' he replied, 'and they are not for you to know. But when the Holy Spirit has come upon you, you will receive power and will tell people about me everywhere—in Jerusalem, throughout Judea, in Samaria, and to the ends of the earth.' (NLT).

89 Lord, A.,: *Spirit, Kingdom and Mission: A Holistic Charismatic Missiology* (Milton Keynes: Paternoster, 2005).

90 Greenslade, P., and Selwyn Hughes, *Cover to Cover: God's Story* (Farnham: CWR, 2001).

91 Marshall, P., *Thine is the Kingdom* (London: Marshall, Morgan and Scott, 1984).

92 Green, F., and Debra Green, *City Changing Prayer* (Eastbourne: Kingsway, 2005).

93 Greig, P., and Dave Roberts, *Red Moon Rising* (Eastbourne: Kingsway, 2004).

94 Greig, P., *The Vision and the Vow* (Eastbourne: Kingsway, 2005).

95 Greig, P. and Andy Freeman, *Punk Monk: New Monasticism and the Ancient Art of Breathing* (Ventura, Regal Books, 2007).